The Second Co

Theory Redux

Series editor: Laurent de Sutter

Published Titles

Franco Berardi, *The Second Coming*

Alfie Bown, *The Playstation Dreamworld*

Laurent de Sutter, *Narcocapitalism*

Roberto Esposito, *Persons and Things*

Graham Harman, *Immaterialism*

Helen Hester, *Xenofeminism*

Srećko Horvat, *The Radicality of Love*

Dominic Pettman, *Infinite Distraction*

Nick Srnicek, *Platform Capitalism*

The Second Coming

Franco 'Bifo' Berardi

polity

Copyright © Franco Berardi 2019

The right of Franco Berardi to be identified as Author of this Work has been asserted in accordance with the UK Copyright, Designs and Patents Act 1988.

First published in 2019 by Polity Press

Polity Press
65 Bridge Street
Cambridge CB2 1UR, UK

Polity Press
101 Station Landing
Suite 300
Medford, MA 02155, USA

All rights reserved. Except for the quotation of short passages for the purpose of criticism and review, no part of this publication may be reproduced, stored in a retrieval system or transmitted, in any form or by any means, electronic, mechanical, photocopying, recording or otherwise, without the prior permission of the publisher.

Extract from *Another Time*, Copyright © 1940 by W.H. Auden, renewed
Reprinted by permission of Curtis Brown, Ltd.

ISBN-13: 978-1-5095-3483-8
ISBN-13: 978-1-5095-3484-5 (pb)

A catalogue record for this book is available from the British Library.

Library of Congress Cataloging-in-Publication Data

Names: Berardi, Franco, author.
Title: The second coming / Franco Berardi.
Description: Cambridge ; Medford, MA : Polity Press, 2019. | Series: Theory redux
Identifiers: LCCN 2018027017 (print) | LCCN 2018041502 (ebook) | ISBN 9781509534852 (Epub) | ISBN 9781509534838 (hardback) | ISBN 9781509534845 (pbk.)
Subjects: LCSH: End of the world--Philosophy. | Civilization, Modern--Philosophy.
Classification: LCC BL503 (ebook) | LCC BL503 .B47 2019 (print) | DDC 303.4--dc23
LC record available at https://lccn.loc.gov/2018027017

Typeset in 12.5/15 Adobe Garamond by
Servis Filmsetting Ltd, Stockport, Cheshire
Printed and bound in Great Britain by CPI Group (UK) Ltd, Croydon

The publisher has used its best endeavours to ensure that the URLs for external websites referred to in this book are correct and active at the time of going to press. However, the publisher has no responsibility for the websites and can make no guarantee that a site will remain live or that the content is or will remain appropriate.

Every effort has been made to trace all copyright holders, but if any have been overlooked the publisher will be pleased to include any necessary credits in any subsequent reprint or edition.

For further information on Polity, visit our website:
politybooks.com

Contents

How To   1
1 In Retrospect   9
2 Apocalypse   49
3 Is There Life after the Apocalypse?   110

Notes   142

How To

How To Deal with Chaos

Those who wage war against chaos will be defeated because chaos feeds upon war.

Chaos does not exist in nature, it is not an objective reality: it is the relation between the human mind and the speed of events that are relevant to our physical and psychological survival.

If we feel as though we are living in conditions of chaos, this means that our minds are unable to emotionally process and rationally decide about events whose speed is intensifying, about proliferating nervous stimulation.

What is the relation between chaos and conscious subjectivity? In the domain of Enlightenment philosophy, conscious subjectivity was expected to reduce chaos to rational order. But today all attempts to govern chaos seem doomed to fail, as info-nervous stimulation has intensified beyond the limits of conscious processing.

Chaos is the measure of the complexity of the world in relation to the capacities of intellectual reduction. From a different angle, chaos is the measure of the excessive density of the infosphere in relation to the psychosphere.

As chaos is fed by war, every attempt to overcome chaos by waging war against it is doomed to failure: fighting terrorism ends up reinforcing it, security campaigns result in increasing insecurity, and legal battles against fake news only lead to the multiplication of shitstorms.

So, finally, what should be done in situations of chaos? Let's read what Deleuze and Guattari say about the subject: 'the struggle against chaos does not take place without an affinity with the enemy'.[1]

When chaos invades the mind and swallows up social behaviour, we should not be afraid of it, and we should not try to subjugate chaos to any order whatsoever. It does not work, as chaos is stronger than order. So the best thing to do is to make friends with chaos. Only inside the whirlwind will the clue to the new rhythm be found.

Wu wei.

Not Action but Interpretation

It may be that Marx's famous eleventh thesis on Feuerbach – the central pillar of the revolutionary methodology of the last century and a half – simply needs to be overturned. Marx wrote there that 'Philosophers have hitherto only *interpreted* the world in various ways; the point is to *change* it'[2] – and the philosophers of the last century tried to do so. The results are catastrophic.

The philosophers' task is not to change the world – the world continually changes with no need of philosophers. The philosophers' task is to interpret the world, that is, to capture its tendency and above all to enunciate the possibilities inscribed therein.

This is the philosophers' primary task: deciphering possibilities. The politician's eye does not see the possible, being attracted instead by the probable. And the probable is no friend of the possible: the probable is the gestalt that allows us to see what we already know, and at the same time prevents us from seeing what we do not know and yet what is right there, in front of our eyes.

Interpretation is the condition for finding the thread that helps us untie the knot, the thread that gives us the ability to escape the labyrinth.

The knot is capitalism, and my thread is the tendency towards reduction of necessary labour time thanks to the increasing connection of the general intellect. How to translate this tendency into an active process of labour-time reduction? This is my labyrinth, and in order to wriggle our way out of the labyrinth, interpretation is needed.

In 'The Fragment on Machines', Marx emphasizes not action, but interpretation.[3] He wants to unfold what is implied, and to transcribe what is inscribed, in the present: the possible. And he reads its tendency by inspecting the entrails of the relationship between knowledge, technology and labour time. This tendency we have to make visible, by force of interpretation.

Black Out

This book is a sort of philosophical account of the year 2017, when chaos, pain and fakery sprawled over planet Earth.

The crumbling of the neoliberal illusion paved the way for the comeback of the obsession with identity politics, but the effects of the illusion, entrenched in the dictatorship of finance, outlived the disillusionment.

Even if the majority of people have realized that the dictatorship of finance has shocked Western democracy and pushed many of the population into destitution and despair, finance is not relaxing its grip.

Aggressiveness, brutality, racism and war are the outcome of the deadlock.

A blackout on sensibility is one effect of this social stranglehold. Idiocy is spreading worldwide as a revolt against the mathematical rationality of financial plundering: a blackout on reason, as revenge does not listen to reasons.

The end of history, which once upon a time was expected to result from the realization of historical Reason (*absolute Vernunft*), has taken the mathematical shape of financial code.

No way out of the abstract violence of the digital capture of experience and language seems viable. So the destruction of modern rationality returns as the only way, and we know (from past experience) that this destruction is self-defeating.

Universal reason has humiliated and paralysed individuals, so individuals resort to the particularity of belonging, identity and race. So came the darkest of nights.

According to Crispin Sartwell:

> it is now painfully clear that we've overestimated intelligence as a world-changing force; it is idiocy that holds sway . . . The traditional culmination of a philosophy of history is to identify the goal, end or destination of the whole human saga. I speculate that the Trump–Kim dialectic is the final stage, in which history simultaneously realises and annihilates itself, and us with it.[4]

Reason is no more the master of our destiny, that's crystal clear.

No more does will seem to be the master of the course of events, notwithstanding the pretentious affirmations of the late modern *Wille zur Macht*.

Since Machiavelli declared that political power (the Prince) is based on the violent submission of the capricious feminine side of reality (whose Latin name is *fortuna*),[5] modern history has been above all a permanent manly war against femininity. At the end of the modern parabola, *fortuna* ('hazard') has grown too rich, too complex and too unpredictable, and the Prince is impotent. Rational government is replaced by techno-linguistic automatisms, and *Will zur Macht* is replaced by impotent rage and aggressive revenge.

War against women is raging in the sexual, religious and economic fields.

The impotence of reason and will is announcing the twilight of his-tory and the shift towards her-story.

Her-story should not be intended as a compensation for past violence, or as a recognition of the role played by women in his-tory (the patriarchal history based on the obsession with power that women have supported with their exploitation and subjugation), but as a different conception of our relation to the unfolding of time: dissipation rather than accumulation, circularity rather than linearity, becoming-other rather than identity, and, last but not least, frugality rather than unlimited growth.

Her-story implies a resizing (namely, a downsizing) of human will, in comparison with the untameable forces of nature and of the unconscious. Her-story means a relativization of the presumed omnipotence of the human will, and a relaxation of the sense of guilt that is linked to the delusion of free will. Finally, her-story stands for a reconsideration of the importance of human action in evolution.

We must rethink from scratch the relation between subjectivity and evolution, and consequently resize the importance of conscious action and political projects.

In a historical framework, conscious intentional action marks the relation between subjectivity and evolution. But we are no longer dwelling in a historical framework, as far as I can understand.

Taoism suggests that non-action (*wu wei*) is the only reasonable way of relating to evolution. Not a different action, but non-action.

This is the lesson that I have drawn from the events of the year 2016–17, when the lights of history went off.

I

In Retrospect

Fifty Years after Sixty-Eight

Rather than a year, '68 is the name of a mindset which actually prevailed in the world throughout two decades (in Italy, for instance, it lasted from 1960 to 1977).

In this sense, '68 means the opening of the heart and of the brain to the emergence of countless possibilities, the participation of millions in the same process of discovery, experimentation and universal friendship.

In the year 1968 I enrolled as a student at the Faculty of Philosophy of the University of Bologna. A lucky occurrence indeed. I had the chance of experiencing from the inside the process of the awakening and gathering of an explosive force that gave way to the unfolding of the first global movement in history.

Fifty years later, I understand that the meaning of that year (of those years) cannot be reduced to a single line of interpretation. Nevertheless, from my point of view that worldwide student insurrection may be read as the conscious emergence of the general intellect, as the first manifestation of the self-awareness of cognitive labour.

In cultural and political terms these fifty years look like a geological era.

I'm 68 years old now, and I live in the same neighbourhood where I used to dwell as a student and as an activist fifty years ago. Almost nothing has changed in the landscape, except the students. I see them from my window: lonely, watching the screens of their smartphones, nervously rushing to classes, sadly going back to the expensive rooms that their families are renting for them. I feel their gloom, I feel the aggressiveness latent in their depression, I know that their aggressiveness may emerge and express itself under the banner of fascism. Not the old fascism that exploded out of futuristic energy, but the new fascism that results from the implosion of desire, from the attempt to keep panic under control and from the depressive rage of impotence.

We may try to explain in political terms the distance of the present depression from the ebullience of fifty years ago, but political explanations explain very little, because they do not help us to go beyond the ideological surface and to grasp the evolutionary meaning of the mutation. This mutation does not concern ideological orientations or discursive and juridical constructions: left versus right, progressive versus conservative and so on.

This mutation runs deeper than that, and it has to be explained in evolutionary terms much more than in political terms.

In order to fully appreciate this mutation, rather than studying political propensities and aversions, we should focus on the relation between the infosphere and the psychosphere, and (looking at the same problem from a different point of view) between knowledge and consciousness.

Information and consciousness
We might think of 1968 as the peak of human evolution, as the moment in which technology,

knowledge and social consciousness reached the point of maximal convergence.

Since then, technological potency has steadily expanded while social consciousness has decreased proportionately. As a result, technology has increasing power over social life, while society has decreasing power over technology, and is no more able to govern itself.

In the conjuncture that we name '68, social consciousness was expected to take control over technological change and to direct it to the common good. But the contrary happened at that point: the leftist parties and the unions regarded technology as a danger, rather than as an opportunity to master and to proffer in the interests of society. Liberation from work was labelled unemployment, and the left engaged in countering the unstoppable technical transformation.

As the relation between information and consciousness is the focus of my reflection here, I will define information as knowledge objectified in signs and conveyed by media, and I will define consciousness (in this context) as the subjective appropriation, elaboration and sharing of the contents of knowledge.

Since the years '68, and particularly in the

wake of the neoliberal turn, the collective mind of humankind has undergone a deep process of reshaping.

The sphere of objectified knowledge has been enormously enhanced, while available time for conscious elaboration has inversely decreased.

This double dynamics has provoked an explosion of unawareness.

Unawareness does not mean lack of information (ignorance) but systemic downsizing of the subjective conscious assimilation of knowledge.

In the years '68, everybody was expecting a long-lasting process of social emancipation from misery and exploitation. This persuasion was totally wrong, as we now know. Exploitation and misery have not decreased; they have transformed and expanded in many ways.

Today the prevailing expectations are very different, almost opposed. Why? What has broken the expectations of fifty years ago, what has provoked this sort of reversal of imagination?

Let's have a look at the world-scape of that time, then let's have a look at the world-scape of today.

In 1968, the world population was around three and a half billion. Today, it is more than double that, although the birth rate has been slowing in the last decades.

Absolute and relative knowledge

While the literacy rate rose steadily until the end of the past century, and is more or less stagnating in the second decade of the twenty-first century, the same cannot be said of tertiary education.

'Literacy rates grew constantly but rather slowly until the beginning of the twentieth century. And the rate of growth really climbed after the middle of the 20th century, when the expansion of basic education became a global priority.'[1]

In relative terms, tertiary education has been slowly decreasing since 1968, and particularly in the first decade of the new century. In Russia (a country that dramatically changed its course at the end of the past century), the highest level of education has fallen in the last twenty years.[2]

In the year 2008, I happened to be teaching in a school for adults, particularly migrants: they came from Morocco, from Bengal, from Peru and many from the former Soviet Empire.

At the beginning of the year, I used to ask some questions more or less randomly, just to test my students' level of preparation. In a class I met two Moldovan men both named Vladimir, and I asked them five or six questions concerning historical events, popular novels and well-known persons like Napoleon, Lenin and Jesus Christ. The old Vladimir, aged 42, formed in a Soviet Union primary school, replied immediately and correctly to all of my questions. The young Vladimir, aged 19, formed in the years following the collapse of the Soviet school system, did not answer one single question – not even 'How many years ago did Jesus Christ come to life?'

The post-Soviet educational catastrophe, which is not an exception but the extreme manifestation of a general trend, was perfectly epitomized in the performances of the two Vladimirs.

Data concerning the access to tertiary education tell of a slow but steady decline in the rate of education, but these data show only the volume, and not the quality, of education of the new generations of humans.

The quality of education has certainly changed, for the better or for the worse, in the last thirty years, as the neoliberal turn has shaken the structure and functions of the educational system, and has reshaped students' cultural motivations and psychological expectations worldwide.

It's difficult to judge the quality of educational formation in different periods of time. However, as a teacher and as someone who has spent most of his time with students and young people, I can affirm that the average young person is today more informed than the average young person of fifty years ago – but at the same time is much less prepared to express critical views and to choose between cultural and political alternatives. Why so?

Knowledge and dogma

The reason lies in the radical change of educational criteria that resulted from the neoliberal reformation of the school system worldwide.

Europe is a good place to observe the neoliberal turn, because since 1999, after the signature of the Bologna Charter, every European country has engaged in transforming the school system in compliance with the market.

Since then, the reform of the educational system in every European country has been marked by de-financing, cuts, job losses, overall precarization of teaching, privatization, and downsizing of the non-rentable disciplinary fields (so-called humanities).

The leading principle of the reform is the assertion of the epistemological primacy of the economic sphere, and this primacy has turned into the general criterion of education.

In the transition from the bourgeois era of industrial capitalism to the digital financial era of semiocapital, mental energy becomes the main force of valorization. This implies the standardization of the procedures of teaching, resulting in the uniform formatting of the cognitive body. A remarkable consequence of this process has been and is the downsizing and de-financing of the so-called 'humanities'.

The autonomy of universities has been the first victim of the market-oriented reformation. The concept of autonomy had a crucial place in the definition of the modern university. This concept did not only refer to the political independence of the university's choices from the religious and political authorities, but referred also and mainly to the inherent methodology of scientific knowledge and artistic practice. Each field of knowledge was deemed to establish its own laws: conventions, aims, procedures, verification and change.

During the bourgeois era, the university was based on two pillars. The first pillar was the relation of the intellectuals and the city, the ethical and political role of reason.

The second pillar was the autonomy of research and teaching – the autonomy of the process of discovery, innovation, production and transmission of moral, scientific and technical acquisition.

The bourgeois, owner and entrepreneur, was aware that autonomy of knowledge was necessary for achieving productive results. The long process of emancipation from theocratic dogma shaped bourgeois culture and identity throughout modern times.

But the neoliberal forging of *Homo oeconomicus* translated every notion and every act of knowledge into economic terms,[3] leading to the abolition of the autonomy of knowledge. The economy has progressively acquired the central place in the system of knowledge and research, re-enacting the privilege of theocracy in the Middle Ages. Every act of research, of teaching, of learning and of inventing is subjected to economic questions: is it rentable? Is it fostering capital accumulation, is it fulfilling the demands of competition?

Automated brain and demented body
The general trend of the past century, peaking in '68, was a steady expansion of mass education and an explosion of consciousness. The general trend of the post-'68 years is a steady relative decline in higher education, and simultaneously an unprecedented explosion of information resulting from the formation of cyberspace and from the proliferation of media.

Since '68, the content of knowledge has enormously increased and has materialized in technology, increasing the general intellect's productivity, but simultaneously jeopardizing the very conditions of consciousness.

The expansion of the infosphere has forced the acceleration of the mental reaction to info-nervous stimulation. But the critical mind is unable to function in conditions of info-nervous saturation, while the rate of education and the quality of education have fallen and deteriorated.

The outcome of these two trends (expansion of the knowledgeable and collapse of the critical mind) is the fantastic ignorance boom whose effects are exposed in the political history of the Trump age, and in the deterioration of the daily life of the majority of people worldwide.

1968 is the peak of human evolution because in those years consciousness and technology were rising together. Then, after a decade of uncertain oscillation, the year 1977 marked the divergence of those two trends: the expansion of technological knowledge and of technological applications continued steadily and accelerated, while social consciousness declined sharply. In the years 2016 and 2017, while the kingdom of artificial intelligence is being inaugurated, humankind is officially entering the age of dementia. The massive support for racism, nationalism and religious war is the evidence of this fall into dementia of the global mind. I use the expression 'dementia' in a literal sense: separation of the automated brain from the living body, and resulting dementia of the brainless social body.

How to make friends with the automaton
The automaton is growing in interconnectedness and pervasiveness: the brain has been objectified in the computational machine, then separated from the social body, so the social body seems unable to behave in a meaningful way.

The solution for humans is to make friends with the automaton.

But it's hard for society to forge an alliance with the automaton as long as the automaton is programmed according to the antisocial paradigm of capital accumulation. In order to make friends with the automaton, we need to sabotage and reprogram the automaton itself. Where is the energy that is necessary for this task to be found?

This energy may be found in the words of Melissa McEwen, who expresses the exhaustion and moral prostration that haunt millions of cognitive workers worldwide:

> Coding for a couple of hours a day in your spare time isn't the same as coding for 8+ hours a day. Over the past decade it has worn me down. I have regular painful migraines triggered by working long hours. I have the beginnings of arthritis in my neck. I've tried standing desks, balance board desks, treadmill desks, special diets, exercising more before and after work. Doctors, physical therapists, massage therapists of every stripe. I've spent thousands and thousands of dollars. I've hidden it because I was afraid it would make me unemployable. I've worked those long hours in intense pain. Because it's not really 'passion' they are looking for, but people who are merely willing

to endure long hours. They aren't really looking for the person who spends a few hours on the weekend on an open-source project, they are looking for the person who comes home from work and spends all night on it.[4]

Millions of cognitarians, engineers and poets, programmers and artists, may subscribe to the words of Melissa McEwen. The disease of millions of cognitive workers is the condition for the creation of a movement of sabotage and reprogramming of the automaton.

In order to move from disease to active subjectivation, however, we should be able to act like Baron Munchausen, who, having fallen into a ditch, lifted himself up by pulling on his own pigtail. This self-creative act (this invention of something from nothing) is the effect of a movement.

This is why we need a comeback of the energy that sprang up in the year '68.

A Hundred Years after the Soviet Revolution

In the past century, the century that trusted in the mythology of the future, Communism was the only reasonable attempt to avert the unleashing of barbarity and mass murder on a planetary scale, and to start redistributing global wealth so as to avoid the armed revenge of the victims of past and present colonialism.

Unfortunately, the 'realization' of Communism has also been the continuation of the authoritarian political style deeply entrenched in Russian culture, and the enforcing of a totalitarian model of control over social life. The horizon of Communism has been identified with the Russian totalitarian experiment, so the Soviet failure has provoked the failure of Communism worldwide.

The simultaneous defeat of the workers' movement and obliteration of the prospect of Communism – two different events which happened in the same years from different causes, albeit interdependently – have destroyed the common ground that was bringing together the class of industrial workers of the West, and the billions of people who have suffered in the long history of colonization.

Communist internationalism was the only attempt to reconcile the workers of the West and the oppressed population of the Global South, and this attempt has failed.

This is the most dramatic effect of the erasure of the Communist project.

The separation of the Western working class from the oppressed populations of the colonized countries is resulting nowadays in a political catastrophe that is threatening the very roots of peace.

The populations that suffered and still suffer from the consequences of protracted forms of imperialist exploitation are raging today without any universal political hope, and resort to every possible weapon, including religious suicide, in order to take revenge for the never-ending humiliation that the predators have enforced on them.

Divested of a strategic horizon of social emancipation, unable to recognize exploitation as their common lot and their common ground of identification, Western workers are following nationalist agendas in order to avert the effects of globalization, and resorting to nationalist and racist forms of identification.

The exit from modern capitalism cannot be less than a tragedy, because the knots tied by colonialist violence cannot be loosed without trauma. This has been known since 1914, when the conflict unleashed a geopolitical fight among nationalisms, and paved the way for violent social revolutions.

The extent of the tragedy was not predictable a hundred years ago, and is not fully predictable now. Nevertheless, a hundred years ago the exit from capitalism was conceivable within the anthropological framework of modernity. Nowadays a political exit from capitalism seems unthinkable, as in the new technical and anthropological framework, political decision is replaced by automatic governance. Therefore the end of capitalism tends to be imaginable only as the end of civilization itself.

The words 'postmodern' and 'postcolonial' entered triumphantly into the cultural lexicon in the 1980s, implying that a peaceful exit from the general forms of modernity was at hand. It was not, because of the legacy of five hundred years of world exploitation and concentration of wealth by the West: devastation of the environment, impoverishment of social life and systematic aggression on the psychosphere.

The large-scale use of the prefix 'post' since the 1980s has tried to evade the tragic toll demanded by the mutation that follows the technological transformation.

The Soviet Revolution was conceived as an exit from modern capitalism (not from the anthropological model of modernity).

A hundred years after the Soviet Revolution, as we ponder the consequences of its final defeat, we cannot escape the perception of spiralling chaos in the geopolitical and in the social fields.

The darkest of nights is falling over the planet: from the Philippines, where Rodrigo Duterte invites the soldiers to rape not more than three women and kill people who are suspected of being drug dealers,[5] to the India of the nationalist Narendra Modi, to Turkey, where thousands of teachers have been fired by the Islamo-fascist dictator, to Hungary, and Poland, to the United States to the United Kingdom – we are facing different degrees of authoritarianism, racism and violence. Is there a way out? Is there a way back to democracy? I don't think so.

A rollback of the aggressive obnubilation of the global mind is unimaginable at the present, and the eradication of the social conditions that led to the spread of hatred seems presently impossible.

Let's face it. The collapse of democracy has been prepared by forty years of neoliberal competition.

Someone said in '68: 'Socialisme ou barbarie.' It was not a *jeu de mots*, but a lucid prediction.

1914 and 1917

During the First World War, Lenin made two daring moves. The first move he made in Zimmerwald in 1914. The war was starting, and German and French socialists voted for war credits in the parliaments of their conflicting nation states, so betraying the internationalist creed for the sake of national interest.

Lenin said 'No' to this betrayal and broke with the Second International.

This move marked the beginning of the history of Communism in the twentieth century.

The second move came in April 1917 when Lenin, returning to Russia, launched the Bolshevik Revolution with the words: 'All power to the Soviet.'

In this second move is rooted the catastrophe of Communism in the century, because this move identified socialism with a nation state and obliged the proletarians of the world to imagine the revolution within national borders and to conceive their autonomy in national terms.

In 1914, Lenin had gone beyond the political

rationale of the modern nation state, beyond Machiavelli and Hobbes. Breaking with the national compromise of the socialist parties of Germany and France, the author of the book *Imperialism, the Highest Stage of Capitalism* opened the way to a process of unification of industrial workers with the colonized peoples of the world, a process of slow dissolution of nations aimed at the formation of the post-national self-government of international workers.

In 1917, however, Lenin went back to the established rules of the nation state, and turned the autonomous interest of the working class into the establishment of a nation state. International class struggle, at that point, was subjected to the interests of socialism in one country alone, and reduced to the logic of national wars.

When in the 1960s and 1970s a new possibility emerged of the common uprising of the oppressed and the exploited of the world, the legacy of the Soviet Revolution played an ambiguous role, obliging the movement to repeat the Leninist attempt and the Leninist failure. The legacy and the memory of Bolshevism led the students and workers of the '68 global insurrection to focus mainly on political assault against the state, missing the opportunity for a post-political action of appropriation of knowledge and technology.

Following the worldwide collapse of Communism, Lenin's legacy has completely dissolved, and we have lost simultaneously the memory of 1914 and of 1917.

Global civil war
In 2016, in the wake of the crisis of globalization, while the British were voting for Brexit and the Americans were listening to Trump, Zbigniew Brzezinski published an article titled 'Toward a Global Realignment':

> Periodic massacres of their not-so-distant ancestors by colonists and associated wealth-seekers largely from western Europe (countries that today are, still tentatively at least, most open to multiethnic cohabitation) resulted within the past two or so centuries in the slaughter of colonized peoples on a scale comparable to Nazi World War II crimes: literally involving hundreds of thousands and even millions of victims. Political self-assertion enhanced by delayed outrage and grief is a powerful force that is now surfacing, thirsting for revenge, not just in the Muslim Middle East but also very likely beyond.

Many of the data cannot be precisely established, but taken collectively, they are shocking. Just a few examples suffice. In the 16th century, due largely to disease brought by Spanish explorers, the population of the native Aztec Empire in present-day Mexico declined from 25 million to approximately one million. Similarly, in North America, an estimated 90 percent of the native population died within the first five years of contact with European settlers, due primarily to diseases. In the 19th century, various wars and forced resettlements killed an additional 100,000. In India from 1857 to 1867, the British are suspected of killing up to one million civilians in reprisals stemming from the Indian Rebellion of 1857. The British East India Company's use of Indian agriculture to grow opium then essentially forced on China resulted in the premature deaths of millions, not including the directly inflicted Chinese casualties of the First and Second Opium Wars. In the Congo, which was the personal holding of Belgian King Leopold II, 10–15 million people were killed between 1890 and 1910. In Vietnam, recent estimates suggest that between one and three million civilians were killed from 1955 to 1975.

As to the Muslim world in Russia's Caucasus,

from 1864 and 1867, 90 percent of the local Circassian population was forcibly relocated and between 300,000 and 1.5 million either starved to death or were killed. Between 1916 and 1918, tens of thousands of Muslims were killed when 300,000 Turkic Muslims were forced by Russian authorities through the mountains of Central Asia and into China. In Indonesia, between 1835 and 1840, the Dutch occupiers killed an estimated 300,000 civilians. In Algeria, following a 15-year civil war from 1830 to 1845, French brutality, famine, and disease killed 1.5 million Algerians, nearly half the population. In neighboring Libya, the Italians forced Cyrenaicans into concentration camps, where an estimated 80,000 to 500,000 died between 1927 and 1934.

More recently, in Afghanistan between 1979 and 1989 the Soviet Union is estimated to have killed around one million civilians; two decades later, the United States has killed 26,000 civilians during its 15-year war in Afghanistan. In Iraq, 165,000 civilians have been killed by the United States and its allies in the past 13 years. (The disparity between the reported number of deaths inflicted by European colonizers compared with the United States and its allies in Iraq and Afghanistan may be due in part to the technological advances that have resulted in the more productive use of force and in part as well to a shift in the world's normative climate.) Just as shocking as the scale of these atrocities is how quickly the West forgot about them.[6]

I know, the quotation is long, but it deserves to be read, because it reminds us that debts are to be paid: not only financial but also historical debts, whose repayments are harsher.

What Brzezinski is describing here, in incredibly daring words, is the background of a sort of apocalyptic endgame: the humiliated of the past are now taking revenge for the past humiliation. The army of the avengers is strong: hundreds of millions of young unemployed who have been promised democracy and welfare and have actually received war and misery. They have nothing to lose except their lives, and they are willing to give their lives away in exchange for revenge, while for the first time in history they have access to weapons of mass destruction.

It's useless to invite those millions of people who are preparing for their final act to reflect rationally and to act in a political way: they just want revenge, and revenge has little to do with reason.

IN RETROSPECT

Some call it 'Dark Enlightenment', and emphasize the end of democracy as the condition for a neo-reactionary self-assertion of the right of the strongest.

With Foucault we may retrace the genealogy of modern reason through the description of the nomination and segregation of unreason.[7]

The Enlightenment is the process of the realization of reason, but reason has been captured by the economy and turned into the rationale of the financial domination of the world. Financial domination has destroyed the lives of countless people, and those people react, rejecting reason. So the neoliberal subjugation of reason has led to the Dark Enlightenment, in which the forces of darkness are now thriving.

The ascent of Donald Trump is understandable in the framework of a sort of white supremacist backlash fuelled by the fear of decline and by the perception of a spreading, global civil war.

White workers, impoverished in the decades of centre-left liberal hegemony, are now revolting against democracy and against globalism.

As long as the conflict opposes neoliberal globalists to anti-global nationalists, it will spiral, with devastating consequences for social life and for peace. Only the emergence of a third actor, that is, conscious solidarity among workers beyond the limits of nations, may dispel the final catastrophe.

As far as we can predict, this emergence is impossible.

Nevertheless, in the words attributed to John Maynard Keynes, the unavoidable does not generally happen because the unpredictable prevails.

It's easy to see the unavoidable, today: the third world war unfolding in a way that is different from the previous two, and the techno-media complex controlling the hyper-connected mind.

Not a fight between imperialist potencies, but a widespread civil war opposing clans, tribes, populations and religious faiths under the umbrella of an insatiable thirst for revenge. At another level, the secluded sphere of automation is ceaselessly pervading and wiring the social brain.

The interests of the white workers of the crumbling West are increasingly diverging from those of the emerging migrants, refugees and unemployed of the countries of the Global South.

As this stalemate is a consequence of the dissolution of internationalism, only a comeback of internationalist consciousness (quite unlikely at present) might avert the apocalyptic prospect that is looming.

No political decision will remove the legacy of colonization.

What we can do is create the conditions for post-apocalyptic times. The first task in this view is to get free from the mythology of 1917 while distinguishing between Lenin in Zimmerwald and Lenin in Petrograd.

Is Fascism Back?

Macro fascism was based on the imitation of a mythological personality embodying the desire of heroism and unity of the nation. In micro fascism the authoritarian spirit is internalized, so micro-fascists do not need a mythological leader, they only need a model of behaviour which may give them the illusion of being in control of everything, mimicking potency they do not have anymore.

In nano-fascism there is neither a figure nor a model left; following a biological mutation, all the specifications that go into the making of a fascist come ready-at-hand in a box, and after a certain period of incubation, they permeate the body down to all of its nano units.[8]

In *Die Schuldfrage* (1946) Karl Jaspers, the philosopher who is credited with being one of the founders of the existentialist movement, suggested a distinction between Nazism as a historical event and the concept of Nazism, the essential meaning of Nazism as a universal phenomenon.[9]

Historical Nazism is a unicum that cannot happen again, but the social and psychological dynamics that gave rise to Nazism in the past century have very much to do with contemporary social dynamics and the contemporary unconscious.

Jaspers wrote that the quintessential feature of Nazism is techno-totalitarianism, and he argued that a full manifestation of the nature of Nazism might re-emerge as a consequence of the full implementation of technology. Günther Anders expressed a similar concept in his writings, particularly in 'We, Sons of Eichmann'. In a ghastly passage he writes:

> we can expect that the horrors of the Reich to come will vastly eclipse the horrors of yesterday's Reich. Doubtless, when one day our children or grandchildren, proud of their perfect 'co-mechanization', look down from the great heights of their thousand

year reich at yesterday's empire, at the so-called 'third' Reich, it will seem to them merely a minor, provincial experiment.[10]

In the year 2017, this appalling prediction seems to be within sniffing distance. We may ignore it, we may ignore the spread of nationalism and racism, and the proliferation of Hitler's imitators like Modi of India, Duterte of Manila and Trump of America, but denial will not help. Nazism seems to be back, in the brutal form of white supremacism, or under the cynically refined guise of Dark Enlightenment.

So it's time to read what Anders wrote fifty years ago about Auschwitz and Hiroshima. According to him, the inmost feature of Nazism was the rationale of extermination perfected by technology: what Auschwitz and Hiroshima have revealed, according to Anders, is that in a techno-civilization inhuman tasks do not need human perpetrators any more:

> in an industrial civilization unhuman tasks increasingly become tasks without humans. The dropping of the atomic bomb on Hiroshima became a paradigm of this to Anders: at the touch of a button,

hundreds of thousands of people were killed in just a few seconds. However, Anders saw the initial attempts to achieve such a mechanization of death in the National Socialists' extermination machinery.[11]

The mechanization of extermination is the essential contribution of Nazism, and the mechanization of extermination is a project that nowadays may be implemented on a much larger scale than in the age of Hitler.

Anders emphasizes the continuity between Auschwitz and Hiroshima as a specific expression of the civilizational development of the modern age.

Since Auschwitz, the machine of extermination has undergone a process of automation, and extermination has turned into an institutionalized task: 'Those employed in the extermination camps did not act, but, as terrible as it may sound, they worked.'[12]

The atomic bomb marked the beginning of a new era:

For the first time in human history, mankind had to envisage the end of the human race as a real possibility. Thus the 'end time' has begun, an era that must anticipate the possibility of the 'end of time', a 'world without human beings' – a possibility about which philosophy too cannot be ultimately indifferent.[13]

When technology takes hold of the war and war takes hold of technology, we are no longer masters of our own technical inventions. The industrialization of extermination implies that humans are taken into an automated project that no one can stop any more. The triumph of technology has led to our world reaching such an enormous magnitude that it has ceased to be really 'ours' in any psychologically verifiable sense. It has led to our world becoming 'too much' for us.

What technological potency allows men to do now is bigger than anything we can fathom. An abyss has opened up between our technical capacity to manufacture and our capacity to conceptualize, and it is growing every day; our capacity to manufacture is unlimited, but our ability to predict the implications of networked technology is limited. Our impotence to imagine, to criticize and to choose is deepening as our technological potency, and the growing automation of technological procedures, are expanding.

The convergence between the automation of the technical operation and the crumbling of the social mind – depression, despair, aggressiveness, fascism – is the dangerous core of the apparently unstoppable apocalypse that looms on the horizon.

Human will is increasingly impotent, as technological change disables human ability to govern social concatenations. The potency of political will – both in democratic forms and in authoritarian forms – is outpaced and replaced by a system of techno-linguistic automatisms. Human will is thus reduced to a sort of ersatz or hysterical surrogacy, or simulation.

Fascism is rising as a despairing and demented rebellion against the impotence of the will, against the subjugation of human events to the automaton. But simultaneously the automaton is gaining ground, thanks to the refinement of digital technology: the techno-linguistic automaton results from the intersection between artificial intelligence and big data, and acts as a prescriptive generator of life forms.

The separation of the brain from the body is

the overall effect of this double movement: the brain – the financial brain, the networked brain, the automated brain – is getting connected in a space that is increasingly secluded from the concrete life of the social body, and therefore inaccessible to the action of human beings.

Fascism will never reappear in its past historical form, but some features of the fascist experience – in both the Italian baroque and the German Gothic fashions – may resurface, and are actually resurfacing today, in a different context. In the last ten years we have experienced a social process that is very similar to the one that developed in the 1920s in Italy and Germany, notwithstanding the differences of the cultural and technological context.

Nowadays, in the second decade of the twenty-first century, if we listen to public discourse worldwide – from the India of Modi to the United States of Trump, to the Hungary of Orbán, to the Poland of Kaczyński and the United Kingdom of Theresa May – we hear the same message: 'Do not think of yourselves as defeated, impoverished workers; think of yourselves as white warriors (Hindu warriors, Islamic warriors), and you will win.' They will not win, but they are poised to destroy the world. We can easily predict that the workers of the world, turned into identitarian warriors, will not win. The promises of Trump to the workers and unemployed of the United States will not be fulfilled. In fact, he has betrayed his promises since day one, when the new US president chose three functionaries of Goldman Sachs and placed them in key positions in the US government, then passed a fiscal reform that would further enhance inequality.

Conditions for American workers will not improve under the Trump administration. So what will happen, what will be the next step? When people realize that Trump does not fulfil his promises, scapegoats will be identified and a finger pointed at them as the enemy. In the United States, scapegoats are easy to find: Muslims, blacks and Latinos are targeted by the election-winning Ku Klux Klan. In Europe, the scapegoats are asylum seekers and the undocumented people who come from Africa and the Middle East.

Impotence, supremacism and the new face of racism
In spite of what I have written in the preceding pages, I do not think that that fascism is back. Not

the original brand of fascism, at least. What we are experiencing today is a return of supremacist mythology, but the anthropological substance has deeply changed. In the Futurist period, in fact, fascism was the aggressive manifestation of the potency of young males who felt marginalized by the bourgeoisie: their style was buoyant, euophoric, and their brutality bore the mark of visionary faith in the future. The contemporary wave of nationalism and racism is fuelled by the sense of despair, humiliation and rage of impotent old white people in the age of globalization.

As far as I know, the concept of humiliation has never been thematized or analysed in the sphere of political thought. What is humiliation, after all?

I would say that 'humiliation' is felt when people are forced to become aware of their inability to fulfil their self-image. Humiliation means breaking down the relationship between self-image, expectation, perceived reality and recognition. White Western workers have been humiliated by neoliberal governance and by the centre-left governments that have been the enforcers of that governance. Western workers have been so humiliated that they have decided to identify themselves no longer as workers but in a different way: as the white race. So the white race is coming back: the 'superior' race, the race of predators.

The sentiment of superiority, unmentionable but deeply entrenched in the Western unconscious and culture, has been contradicted and humiliated by the reality of financial capitalism, by the daily experience of impotence that has destroyed people's self-esteem and trust in the future.

The *Futurist Manifesto* of 1909 was an exaltation of sexual potency and political aggressiveness, and fascism drew its force from the mythological virility of Mussolini. Furthermore, historical fascism was the expression of a true sense of belonging: the sense of community was based on the mythology of blood and nation, but the community in those days was something real, daily experienced and deeply moulding social behaviour.

The postmodern return of fascism is based on a completely different anthropology. Community is only a nostalgic memory of a past condition of belonging that exists no longer. Regret, not a living experience. Social life has been pulverized in the metropolitan, post-political, deterritorialized space, and potency is but a myth, a counterpoint to present impotence. Sexual potency is declining, as the majority of the white population is ageing, and stress, depression, angst disturb the erotic sphere. The autonomy of women has been the ultimate threat to vanishing masculine power, and has fuelled a repressed sentiment of macho revenge that erupts more and more often in acts of violence.

Demography has transformed the anthropological and social landscape of our time: senility, loneliness, psychopharmacological addiction are pushing white men in the Western world into mental mayhem, self-contempt, aggressiveness. The new brand of fascism arises not from a juvenile futuristic euphoria but from a widespread sense of depression and an impotent will for revenge.

This trend is especially visible in the US: the depressed multitude of American white men is rooted in the age of rampant individualism: they trusted the promises of neoliberal selfishness, they trusted the philosophy of winning, then discovered losing. They trusted the neoliberal promises of individual success and they were deluded. Now it's too late to embrace a new hope, a new imagination: the only thing they can share is their hatred, their wish for revenge.

This is the anthropological background of Trumpism. 'Make America great again' is a pathetic supplication to the Supremacist God: give me back youth, strength, sexual energy, and faith in something. But the Supremacist God is not listening.

The racism of our time is not a continuation of the racist ideology of the colonial age. That old racism was an expression of the superiority of the dominant race that possessed technology for the exploitation, and weapons for the subjugation, of the coloured people of the primitive or underdeveloped Global South. Now weapons are available to everybody, without race distinction.

Now poor white people are obliged to tolerate the overcrowding of their life spaces as migrant people are confined in the indigent suburbs of the metropolis. This new racism is that of the losers.

The old racism was shared by the upper class and by proletarians; it was the mark of the superiority of white colonizers over the global colonized.

Now racism is left to the destitute and the

ignorant, while the upper class is indignant at the racism of the poor and, from the well-protected rich residential areas of the city, looks down at the slums where migrants live, mingling with the marginalized and impoverished.

The official anti-racism of the European upper class is full of hypocrisy and contempt towards those who are obliged to share the space of their disadvantaged areas with migrant people, who never stop coming, provoking a sense of being invaded.

Despite the anthropological difference between historical fascism and the contemporary comeback, a common trait links contemporary Trumpism with the old fascism: the racist cult of supremacy: race is a defining feature of people's self-identification.

Racism emerged in the culture of the European colonizers during the construction of their empire, as an ideological justification of their acts of plunder. In the *Essai sur l'inégalité des races humaines* (1853), Alfred de Gobineau not only asserted the superiority of the white race, but also predicted a tendency towards racial contamination and consequent degradation of the superior race.[14] Notwithstanding the lack of scientific foundation for his theory and for the very concept of race, Gobineau's racist analysis brought to the surface a very deep stream of the Western unconscious: a stream of fear that originates from the awareness of the impending decline of white Western culture. Despite its lack of scientific meaning, the concept of race acts as a phantasmatic self-identification. This identification played a crucial role in the history of modern colonialism, and is playing a new role in the current catastrophe of capitalism.

The ascent of Donald Trump to the presidency of the United States has revealed exactly this: impoverished by the globalization of the labour market, bamboozled by beer and drugs, furious at the strategic defeat provoked by George W. Bush and his malign adviser Dick Cheney, the white race reclaims its stumbling primacy. 'Make America great again' means: make the white race superior again, in the spirit of the Ku Klux Klan, infuriated when a black president (cultured, polite and beautiful, in contrast to the idiotic dumbheads of the KKK) unconscionably occupied the White House.

2

Apocalypse

The Expanding Sphere of Nothingness

Consciousness and nothingness
In the beginning there was matter (magma, chaos, infinite possibilities without form).

Then signification (language) turned matter into form, and chaos into a world of order: provisional order of meaning, projection of subjective forms and transformation of magma into cosmos.

Consciousness is the only place where nothingness exists.

Only a conscious mind can generate the experience of dissolution into nothingness.

The dissolution of a sensible and conscious

organism (what we usually call death) is the disclosure of nothingness.

All that was solid melts into air: from the decomposition of living matter fresh living matter arises, but in the process a meaningful order disappears, as consciousness dissolves into nothingness.

Order is continuously turning into chaos, form is continuously turning back into matter, and we call this transition death.

Paradoxically, the religious assumption that soul is eternal and the body is doomed to disappear, the philosophical assumption that form is eternal and matter is destined to become nothing, nihil, should be reversed: matter is continuously metamorphosing, transferring from a physical being to another physical being. The soul, which belongs to the singularity of a body, is not metamorphosing and moving elsewhere (unless one believes in metempsychosis, which is an interesting subject that goes beyond the limits of this text). The soul is dying, forever, while the body, after decomposition through molecular recombination, transfers into new bodies.

Capitalism has been an attempt to overcome death, and to fix time in a never-ending process of accumulation of dead labour: valorization. The most accomplished and successful attempt to achieve immortality, as far as I know. A sort of frozen immortality of dead labour that captures living labour in an immortal trap. Speaking of the relation between capital and living labour, Marx wrote the sentence: 'Le mort saisit le vif.'

Capitalism is dead, but it has achieved immortality thanks to financial and virtual transubstantiation. The financial mathematization of the ordinary business of life is the source of the immortalization of the corpse of capitalism.

The physical manifestation of capitalism (industrial economy) is subsumed by digital language, as the physical process of production is replaced by info-recombination, and the accumulation of goods is replaced by financial simulation. Multidimensional reality is dissolved into zero-dimensional information. Then artificial intelligence applied to the internet of things gives three-dimensional existence to the products of info-simulation.

Micro-engines of artificial intelligence are built into the infrastructures of daily life, and the digital invades the biosphere, turning chaos into order: the order of abstraction.

APOCALYPSE

The twentieth century has been traversed by a powerful drive towards abstraction.

Ontology has been finally resolved into language, from Carnap to Wittgenstein to Heidegger to Virno.

Money and language are the abstractions that move the world: they are nothing, yet nevertheless they are mobilizing the energy that changes the world.

The Latin word *abstrahere* means 'to drag away, to divert from'. Abstraction therefore is the extraction of nihil from something: the extraction of a mathematical relation from the physical set of phenomena, the extraction of an informational algorithm from a material process. This nihil is functioning.

In the sphere of capitalist production, labour is abstracted from the concrete usefulness of activity. Then capital itself is abstracted from physical assets and the material production of things, and turned into pure mathematical relation: figures, algorithms, deductions.

Bodies proliferate outside the abstract bunker: secluded from the functioning brain of the frozen corpse of capitalism, they act as demented bodies.

In the age of full implementation of the linguistic automaton, nothingness takes the shape of knowledge without consciousness.

Nihilism, at this point, wears the political mask of fascism: demented attempt to resist abstraction.

A growing part of the Euro-American population supports nationalist anti-migration politics and votes for right-wing parties. Journalists and traditional politicians describe them as populists, but the word 'populism' means nothing, is just an attempt to deny reality. Populism, a movement that emerged in the nineteenth century in prevailingly agrarian Russian society, has nothing to do with the present right-wing wave. The word 'populism' mixes together two very different things: the social rejection of financial plundering and the racist rejection of migrants.

Those who vote for the neo-reactionary parties are essentially seeking revenge, and they want to oppose nothing, nihil, to the present power of humiliation. Nihilism is the growing wave of self-contempt and self-destruction, as nihilism is the only possible reaction to the impotence that follows the accomplishment of abstraction.

In the age of accomplished abstraction we dwell in the frozen corpse of capitalism, frantically seeking a way out; and not finding it, we resort to the power of nothingness.

The Empire of Chaos and the Embedded Order

The modern age may be described as a process of emancipation from the laws of nature, a process of domestication. This implied the expansive subjection of the environment to the rules of politics and architecture: the forces of nature have been largely subjected to the project of civilization, and to urban design.

At the exit from modernity, computation has taken the place of all-encompassing nature, and the rules of the automaton seem to be as inescapable as natural laws.

Thomas Hobbes envisioned the state as the rational force which holds in abeyance the natural unbridled violence of men. Thanks to this progressive domestication of the environment, thanks to the ability of the nation state to regulate and shape territory and population, industrial capitalism emerged and channelled social energies towards the common goal of civilization and development.

At the end of modernity, the neoliberal reformation replaced the regulatory force of the disciplinary state with the self-regulating techno-control which is named governance. Power has been embedded in the extrastatecraft space of algorithmically generated infrastructure.

The Leviathan is no longer the state, shaped and directed by the political will of conscious conflicting subjects, but the mathematical rationale inscribed in the financial algorithm and in the technical structure of governance.

Human political will has lost its effectiveness.

Modernity started with an assertion of ontological freedom that is the core of humanism: the human enterprise (*intrapresa*) is not determined by the law of God or by the law of nature, as long as the political will of the Prince is able to subjugate Fortuna.

In chapter 25 of *The Prince*, Machiavelli argues that the Prince is the masculine will that overcomes the feminine, capricious unpredictability of Fortuna (chance).[1] This is the Machiavellian definition of 'politics': the art of subjecting the unpredictable forces of nature to a rational project.

This art is impotent today, in the age of computing and of chaos.

Fortuna has grown too complicated and too unpredictable, so chaotic that the Prince is unable to govern her. So the political prince gives way to the mathematical automaton.

The acceleration of info-flows and the proliferation of media-machines have provoked a chaotic intensification of the sphere of Fortune. The unpredictable grows and the attention span for making decisions in the hyper-world is reduced to micro-seconds. No time for critical assessment, no time for emotional elaboration. Chaos is an effect of intensification.

While chaos spreads in the domain of life, order is embedded in the connective entrails of abstraction.

Does abstraction have entrails? Good question. I will not answer it now.

At the end of modernity a sort of disjunction occurs: on the one hand, intelligence is captured by technology, and artificial intelligence allows the automated replication of social exchanges.

On the other hand, the emotional sphere, detached from technology and divested of the filters of ethical consciousness, goes back to the brutality of aggressive identity: nationalism, racism, religious fanaticism take hold of the destiny of humankind.

After the failure of Communism

Communism was an attempt to rescue consciousness from the automatisms of the beast and of the machine. But the beast and the automaton have gained the upper hand on the contemporary stage, and they are separately expanding, and invading the whole space of social life.

Global civil war is looming as a secular trend: it does not much resemble the past century's world wars. It does not deploy along stable, recognizable lines, and it is proliferating along multiple fronts in unpredictable ways.

A map of the present global civil war shows that the geography of the conflict is continuously changing along overlapping lines of national, religious or ethnic definition.

In the background of worldwide chaos, however, we distinguish the lines of an overall opposition: the conflict between the race of dominators, the colonizers who identify themselves as 'the white race', and the multiple crowd of the colonized (far from being united; rather fragmented in a thousand interweaving conflicts), the multitude of those who have been subjected to white domination for centuries.

No ground of common understanding is in sight: progress, democracy, peace are words that have lost their appeal, their credibility.

Was this outcome avoidable at the end of the modern era?

At a certain point in the late modern age, the Communist internationalist vision tried to overcome national, religious and ethnic divisions, replacing them with the political identification of the exploited workers, consciously united against capitalism.

Communism has been an immense process of the production of self-consciousness in a considerable part of the world's population, and has developed the humanist principles promoting (with disputable success) a universal ethics of egalitarianism.

Internationalism has been the only horizon of friendly social recomposition on a planetary scale, the only platform for a common exit from colonialism.

As Communism has been erased from the imagination of our time, internationalism has everywhere vanished from the popular consciousness, so we are now dealing with a war that has the features of a global, fragmentary civil war, and is marked from the bottom up by the effects of financial globalization.

Since 11 September 2001, we have entered into the sphere of a chaotic process whose general shape is global civil war. The axis of this war counterposes the populations that have been subjected to the colonial order of the past to the white population of the northern hemisphere (including Russia, Japan and what used to be called the West). The social conflict between employers and workers has been cancelled by the precarization of labour and by the ideological offensive of neoliberalism.

The West is vanishing as a geopolitical concept. It was defined from two points of view: from a political perspective, as democracy, in opposition to the non-democratic systems, and above all to the Soviet Empire.

Secondly, it was defined from an economic perspective as the geopolitical sphere of liberal capitalism.

In the age of Trump, the logical borders of the West are disappearing.

It's hard to consider the United States of

America as a model of democracy when the president, elected by a minority of votes (Clinton received three million more votes than Trump), is destroying the rules of democratic life, and unilaterally dismantling the rules of global exchange.

Furthermore, the opposition between Russia and the US, although persisting and worsening, is no longer the central axis of the global war-scape. This war-scape is following lines of racial and religious identification.

When the war follows religious lines, as in the case of the war against Islamist terrorism, Russians and Americans belong to the same geopolitical area: that of the white Christian race.

The expansion of new capitalist economies all around the globe, the fast growth of many neo-industrialized countries (China, India, South Korea and many others), is cancelling the economic distinction that once upon a time defined the West, as the industrial potencies of the past are losing the force of competition and expansive energy.

At present, we don't have a theoretical model for conceptualizing the current double-faced reality: the order of the technological network and the chaotic proliferation of multi-layered conflicts.

Let's try to sketch the general lines of a descriptive model.

The delusive Empire

At the beginning of this century, in a much-celebrated book written in the wake of the Soviet Union's crumbling, Michael Hardt and Toni Negri shaped a conceptual model intended to cover globalization, democracy and technological transformation. The title of the book is *Empire*.[2]

The emergence of an imperial sphere marks the end of national sovereignty, and the obliteration of any dimension outside capitalism. The implicit assumption was the assimilation of the social landscape to the smooth dimension of the net.

Hardt and Negri's book had the merits of breaking the link with the old dialectical style of thought, and of disavowing any nostalgic attempt to restore the old oppositional conflict between socialism and capitalism on a national basis.

Thanks to that book, we have come to understand that globalization cannot be criticized or subverted by the national sphere of sovereignty. The nation state has lost its effectiveness because of the globalization of the technical conditions of social reproduction, and because of the marriage of digital technology and financial governance.

This is the reason why *Empire* has been important: as a political reframing of critical thought. Nevertheless, over fifteen years after the book's publication we must acknowledge that very little of that text is still useful for understanding something of the present reality of the world.

On the first page of *Empire* we read the following words:

> Along with the global market and global circuits of production has emerged a global order, a new logic and structure of rule, in short a new form of sovereignty. Empire is the political subject that effectively regulates these global exchanges, the sovereign power that governs the world.

Hardt and Negri saw the interdependence of political sovereignty and technical coherence of the system as the source of its fundamentally peaceful order:

> Finally, we should note that an idea of peace is at the basis of the development and expansion of

Empire. This is an immanent idea of peace that is dramatically opposed to the transcendent idea of peace, that is, the peace that only the transcendent sovereign can impose on a society whose nature is defined by war. Here, on the contrary, nature is peace.[3]

The Leviathan portrayed by Hobbes was the external force of imposition of a political order over the natural *bellum omnium contra omnes*. But now, thanks to the biopolitical pervasiveness of the networked machine, according to Hardt and Negri, the nature of global sovereignty is peace.

Hardt and Negri's theoretical illusion, the illusion of the peaceful nature of the new global form of capitalism, descends from the overlapping of world order and networked order. This illusion was fostered by the neoliberal triumph of the 1990s, and was based on the identification of social evolution with the spread of a technical globalizing network.

This identification proved false: war re-emerged after September 11, then the economic cycle turned chaotic after the crisis of 2008.

Now, in the second decade of the twenty-first

century, globalization is contested by the re-emerging forces of nationalism, and the Empire has vanished, replaced by the banners of America First.

This does not imply that globalization has actually been reversed. It has not.

This does not mean that nation states have regained political and economic sovereignty. They have not.

The nation state, which in the second part of the past century was the guarantor of social welfare and was supposed to redistribute resources, has changed its nature, turning into the enforcer of financial governance, the promoter of the systematic subjection of social activity to the repayment of infinite debt.

The concept of Empire misses the crucial point: the uncoupling of the global networked process of production and governance (the supposed Empire) from the action of the living social body of the planet and humankind, which manifests itself in the geopolitical and social unmaking of any order, in the unleashing of conflicting identities, in the spiral of chaos.

Seventeen years after the beginning of the endless war started by Osama bin Laden and

George W. Bush, the American Empire is in tatters. The most powerful army of all time is paralysed, unable to win, unable to quit, unable to negotiate.

Afghanistan, Iraq, North Korea have shown that military predominance does not at all translate into political government.

Hardt and Negri's interpretation is based on the assumption that biopolitical networks and institutional systems converge to the point of overlapping. These authors write, in fact:

> The fundamental object that the imperial relations of power interpret is the productive force of the system, the new biopolitical and institutional system.[4]

This assumption is wrong.

The geopolitical landscape changed enormously in the first decade of the new century, but not in the direction of lasting peace and a long economic boom.

Since the collapse of the net economy that, in the year 2000, provoked the dissolution of the dot.com economy and paved the way for the corporatization of the digital sphere, the US has entered a cycle of military self-defeat and intellectual bankruptcy.

In 1998, asked by a journalist about American support for bin Laden against the Soviet invaders, Brzezinski replied that Islam was not a danger comparable to that posed by the Soviet Union.

It was only partially true. The Soviet Union was a political enemy, but Islam's menace runs deeper. The Soviet Union challenged the West on a social and political basis, but the anthropological (and religious) roots of Western modernity were not threatened by Russian Communists.

The challenge of Islam concerns the anthropological dimension of culture, and questions the supremacy of the white race, the colonizers, who share a Christian background.

The infinite war that erupted after September 11 with the proclaimed goal of fighting terrorism has turned into a sort of showdown of five hundred years of colonialism.

The terrorist action of al Qaeda was not motivated as an act of anti-colonialism: far from it. In the consciousness of the militants who launched the aeroplanes against the World Trade Center, there was a strategic project and a religious motivation very distant from an anti-colonial consciousness. Nevertheless, the events that followed the terrorist action – war in Afghanistan, war in Iraq, then the spread of jihadist suicidal terrorism – show the effects of a long colonial humiliation.

The strategic defeat of the world's most powerful nation is to be viewed in the framework of the long-lasting effects of colonial humiliation and of the inability of Western political culture to come to terms with the crumbling of the modern order, and of colonial rule.

Despite the unquestionable value of Hardt and Negri's repositioning of perspective (rejection of any return to national sovereignty, assertion of the non-opposability of globalization), their book is essentially flawed when it comes to outline a model of interpretation.

The new century has totally disclaimed the descriptive model contained in *Empire*, and the history of the world has taken a path totally different from the one that Hardt and Negri outlined in their book.

They speak of the 'transformation of the global frontier into an open space of imperial sovereignty', and write of the 'birth of a new world order',[5] but the events that occurred just after the book's publication tell a totally different story. The new world order has turned into the dissolution of any political order, and the Empire has turned into what Alain Joxe defined as *L'empire du chaos* in a 2002 book.[6]

Empire of chaos in the place of new world order.

Nevertheless, global capitalist production and financial accumulation are not disintegrating at all: on the contrary, their potency is enhanced and their energy unleashed. How is it possible? How can the capitalist machine keep perfectly together, how can social life deploy productively, inside the Empire of chaos?

I don't think that we have a logical paradox here. We must distinguish the level of life, invaded by chaotic flows that make political will impotent, from the level of abstract governance, from the technical functioning of the global machine ruled by the mathematical logic of techno-financial abstraction.

Those two levels are distinct, even if networked abstraction pervades the entire fabric of daily life.

Extrastatecraft

In 1978 Simon Nora and Alain Minc published a report titled *L'informatisation de la société*.[7] In the text (commissioned by the then French president, Valéry Giscard d'Estaing) the engineer Nora and the sociologist Minc envision a future transformation based on the concatenation of telephone networks and computing machines, and they name this concatenation 'telematics'.

The effect of telematics, they say, will be the disempowerment of the nation state. Media flows and financial flows will evade national borders, so that national jurisdiction will fall short of the ability to control the effects of this technical change.

The history of the last forty years has largely proved this prediction true.

Nevertheless, we may say that the nation state has not disappeared; it has rather been reconfigured.

The social function of the state has been almost cancelled by the neoliberal reformation. In the second half of the twentieth century, the state was an agent of redistribution of wealth, and the source of welfare for the unpriviledged class. The first goal of the neoliberal reformation has been the dismantling of the welfare state, blamed for the loss of competitive strength in global markets.

When the market gained the upper hand over the social good, deregulation prepared the subjection of social life to systemic financial plunder.

This plundering has been incorporated into a system of financial and economic rules and has transformed the organization of labour worldwide, enabling the deterritorialization of the production process.

Financial corporations establish the rules of the game, and networked governance inscribes those rules in the social economy, forcing workers to work more and be paid less in favour of capital accumulation. In this new dimension, the nation state is performing a new task: it is now the enforcer of the permanent transfer of social resources to the banking system.

The nation state has survived by transforming its role into something quite different from that of the past: no more the guarantor of social welfare, it has turned into the guarantor of financial profit.

This new system, however, is not enforced by political persuasion or by the law, although the reformulation of the international rules of trade has been a constant preoccupation of the global corporations. The enforcement of the new 'deregulated' regulation is essentially embodied in the technical infrastructure of communication. Techno-linguistic automatism is implemented by the physical network of the telematic infrastructure.

In the 2015 book *Pax Technica*, Philip Howard explains that:

> the internet of things will be the next, immense, physical layer of networked devices. We experience the internet through a few kinds of devices and the browsers they support. But the internet of things will be defined by communication between devices more than between people. It will be a different kind of internet: larger, more pervasive, and ubiquitous.[8]

Howard speaks of an empire of connected things: ruling the world is no longer the task of a political intelligence orienting and overlooking human conjunctions and interactions, but the effect of ubiquitous connections that coerce human behaviour and submit any action, any pathway, any choice to the binary substance of networked engines.

In the 2014 book *Extrastatecraft*, Keller Easterling outlines the emergence of integrated, production-oriented zones as a new model of urbanism, in which the city is no longer a living organism interacting with capital, technology and production, but a space of technical infrastructures connecting and preordaining the exploitation of labour in a condition of precariousness, deterritorialization, isolation and ceaseless recombination.[9]

The result of this new organization is the lowering of salaries, the obliteration of social solidarity and of the political autonomy of workers, and finally the impossibility of choosing an alternative, of deciding any systemic change: in a few words, the annihilation of democracy.

Easterling suggests the concept of extrastatecraft infrastructure, and says that power is no longer grounded in laws, or in diplomacy or political decision and military force, but in techno-informational infrastructures that escape the grasp of the state.

> Some of the most radical changes to the globalised world are being written not in the language of law and diplomacy, but in these spatial, infrastructural

technologies . . . infrastructure becomes a medium of what might be called extrastatecraft.[10]

The word 'infrastructure' is not new, of course: it used to refer to the physical, mechanical structures which enable social integration, like electrical wires, railways, airports and oil refineries. Easterling writes that:

> today, more than grids of pipes and wires, infrastructure includes pools of microwaves beaming from satellites and populations of atomized electronic devices that we hold in our hands. The shared standards and ideas that control everything also constitute an infrastructure.[11]

More and more infrastructures tends to be similar to an operating system, a set of instructions and of electronic connections that enable the city to function.

> Infrastructure space, with its power and currency of software, is an operating system for shaping the city.[12]

Easterling is especially interested in describing the new urban creations fostered by the embedding of techno-informational infrastructures. The urbanists and architects who have created the new areas of production and housing are no longer designing cities; they are building zones of recombinant integration. The new urban sites, conceived as hubs of deterritorialized capital, are zones generated by algorithms for the optimization of profit and for the perfect exploitation of deterriorialized, underpaid labour.

Easterling adds:

> Like an operating system, the medium of infrastructure space makes certain things possible and other things impossible.[13]

The infrastructure is becoming something like a disposition, in the Foucauldian sense of 'dispositif'. The construction of codes, programs, standards, connecting engines allows certain uses (while forbidding others) like an embedded prescription.

> The designer of disposition in infrastructure space is a performer.[14]

So the design and the enforcing of social processes are no longer a political task, no longer a problem of legal injunctions and prohibition. Instead they are the embedding of technical and linguistic automatisms in the enablers and connectors of social interactions and of production processes.

Easterling reminds us of a crucial moment in the origin of extrastatecraft, back in the nineteenth century:

> For many historians, the first meeting of the International Telegraph Union in Paris in 1863 may be worthy of no more than an obscure technical footnote. Telegraph networks had been growing throughout Europe, prompting the need for international protocols regarding currency, tariffs, the Morse telegraph platform . . . Telecommunications historian Anton Hurdeman has noted that it was the first international agreement concerning most of Europe since the peace of Westphalia 1648.[15]

The reference to the Peace of Westphalia has a special symbolic significance here, because in the Congress that negotiated the treaties, which opened a period of peace among European countries, the very foundations of the modern nation state were laid. From that moment, the nation state was identified as the place of political and economic sovereignty, and this role of the state went unchallenged until the end of the past century, since when the digital networks have circumvented territorial control, borders, political decisions and the authority of the nation state. This is exactly what Nora and Minc had predicted in the year 1978. The Westphalian order has been shaken: the relevant flows of information, of finance and of immaterial production circulate freely in the post-Westphalian space, and political decision is increasingly unable to check those flows, to the point where national sovereignty is inoperative and political will is impotent to change the course of the economy and to stop the delocalization of labour.

Order is no longer the business of the nation state, and is no longer the effect of a political decision: the post-Westphalian order is based on the embedded system of automatisms that enables the business of daily life.

The problem is that while order is inscribed in the automated technical infrastructure of the networked brain of semiocapital, the social body, separated from the connected brain, infuriated by political impotence and fragmented into cells of affective isolation, is reacting with an aggressive assertion of identity and a suicidal drive.

Hardt and Negri's concept of Empire was outlined in the years of the Clintonian world hegemony. But today the American nation is exploding, and the question that arises in the Trump years is the following: will the United States survive as a state, as a nation, as a political and military potency?

I don't know. What I do know is that while Americans are losing all the wars they provoke, millions of weapons are disseminated in American houses, and the psycho-scape of the American mind looks quite frightening.

Hard times ahead for the US.

But the US is not America.

While the political order of the country is dissolving because of the impotence of democracy, and because of the spreading mental disorder among the US population, the techno-linguistic apparatus is taking over the control of the planet.

FAGMA, the concatenation of the most important semio-corporations (Facebook, Apple, Google, Microsoft, Amazon), is taking the place of the Empire, ensuring the global integration of the planet despite the dissolution of the past political order. FAGMA is the technological expression of the culture that descends from the Puritanical occupation of the North American continent, from the Puritanical passion for destroying every form of human life and of human culture in order to establish the world of binary purity, the new Jerusalem.

America is the utopia of a deterritorialized territory empty of real life, in which simulations can freely proliferate, and bodily impurity has to be removed together with the ambiguity of language.

Dementia of the body and automation of the brain: this is the neuro-totalitarian fabric of the Empire of chaos.

Guns, Opioids and Reason

>I sit in one of the dives
>On Fifty-second Street
>Uncertain and afraid
>As the clever hopes expire
>Of a low dishonest decade:
>Waves of anger and fear
>Circulate over the bright
>And darkened lands of the earth,

> Obsessing our private lives;
> The unmentionable odour of death
> Offends the September night.
> (W. H. Auden, 'September 1939')

On 1 October 2017, fifty-eight people were killed and more than 500 injured by a gunman in Las Vegas.

As the news spread over the airwaves and on the net, the Fox News anchorman (and sexual harasser) Bill O'Reilly boiled the massacre down to six words: 'This is the price of freedom.'

Oh yes, freedom.

Freedom to stockpile weapons, and to order ammo online. Freedom to outfit guns with bump stocks to make them fire faster, as the Vegas shooter did. This is the price of freedom, all right.

When a young man called Kelley, just thirty-four days after Vegas, gunned down twenty-six persons during a church service in Sutherland Springs, Texas, President Trump shrugged away the massacre saying that it had nothing to do with guns, only with mental health.

Oh yes, mental health.

President Trump is an expert on mental health, of course, and a super-expert on mental suffering, as he won the election thanks to the epidemic of depressive rage.

The problem is that mentally disturbed people are no longer an innocent minority of the overall population. Mental suffering is more American than Coca-Cola, more American than the stars and stripes. Mental suffering – depression, anxiety, fear, paranoia, impotent rage and drug addiction – is saturating America's life. That's the point.

Everywhere in the world the rise of neoliberal competition – implying the intensive exploitation of nervous energies – has unleashed an epidemic of mental suffering. In the United States of America, however, because of the violent culture of the country and because of the easy availability of weapons, mental suffering often results in mass murders.

Think of Stephen Paddock, the guy who killed fifty-eight persons, shooting from the window of his four-star Las Vegas hotel. He was a normal guy until the day everybody was obliged to realize that he was a mass murderer.

Let's listen to John Weinreich, an acquaintance of Paddock, who was an executive casino host at the Atlantis Casino Resort Spa in Reno,

Nevada, where Mr Paddock was once a regular and where he met his girlfriend:

> He would sit in front of [the gambling machines] for hours, often wagering more than $100 a hand. The way he played – instinctually, decisively, calculatingly, silently, with little movement beyond his shifting eyes and nimble fingers – meant he could play several hundred hands an hour. Casino hosts knew him well.
>
> 'Not a lot of smiles and friendliness', said John Weinrich . . . 'There was not a lot of body movement except for his hands.' . . .
>
> 'He was a math guy', Eric Paddock, his youngest brother, said. 'He could tell you off the top of his head what the odds were down to a tenth of a percent on whatever machine he was playing. He studied it like it was a Ph.D. thing. It was not silly gambling. It was work.'[16]

The spreading global civil war has little to do with political rationality, persuasion and critique; much more with depression, panic and drug intoxication.

> Chris Christie, whom Trump appointed to lead a commission to study the issue, has compared

opioid-overdose fatalities to terrorist attacks, saying, 'We have a 9/11-scale loss every three weeks.' Opioids, which include prescription painkillers and drugs like heroin and fentanyl, are indeed responsible for large-scale human suffering. According to the National Survey of Drug Use and Health, 97.5 million Americans used, or misused, prescription pain pills in 2015. Drug-overdose deaths have tripled since 2000, and opioid abuse now kills more than a hundred Americans a day. But often omitted from the conversation about the epidemic is the fact that it is also inflicting harm on the American economy, and on a scale not seen in any previous drug crisis.[17]

Drug overdose deaths in 2016 exceeded 59,000, the largest annual jump ever recorded in the United States, according to preliminary data compiled by the *New York Times*. Drug overdoses are now the leading cause of death among Americans under the age of fifty.

Opium is a gift of God, like cannabis and like psilocybin and many other substances that in modern times have been subjected to prohibition and simultaneously transformed into expensive and lucrative goods. The prohibition regime, accompanied by the famous war on drugs of Bush the first, is the condition for massive commodification and transformation of natural pharmacopoeia into industrial exploitation, and widespread intoxication.

Politics and psychopathology have long been considered two distinct fields of investigation. Marxist social critique and Freudian psychoanalysis have been discussed as two distinct theories. In the 1960s and 1970s, the exchanges between those two fields intensified, but recently the two different realms have thoroughly fused. The capture and submission of the social mind by the infosphere intensifies the exploitation of nervous energies and the mobilization of the unconscious.

The ensuing pathology is the living substratum of the crisis of reason that progressive philosophy laments, and of the crisis of politics that leads to the comeback of darkness and slavery.

After the marginalization of unreason that Foucault described in his books, reason was to be king of the modern world.

However, as Adorno and Horkheimer predicted in their famous book on the dialectics of Enlightenment,[18] reason has turned into the enforcer of the fatality of capitalism, so in the end people divorced reason. You can call it Dark Enlightenment if you want: the revenge against reason and the comeback of belonging.

Racism, supremacism and identitarian obsession are the political effects of the psychopathology that is haunting the mind of the senescent white population of the planet, those who in past centuries enjoyed the benefits of colonialism and of the welfare state.

This kind of supremacism of white workers humiliated by financial omnipotence brought Trump to the White House, and is now spreading as the dominant feature of the European unconscious.

Barred for many years from the political discourse of the European elite, the great migration exploded at a certain point as the catalyst of the European unconscious. Infuriated by social impoverishment, by the reduction of wages and the dismantling of social services, unable to find a political way out from the austerity imposed by global finance, the European population is staging a replay of the dark show called fascism. The Mediterranean basin is the scenario of this restaging.

APOCALYPSE

Trumping Truth in the Empire of Fake

Sad is Eros, builder of cities,
And weeping anarchic Aphrodite.
(W. H. Auden, 'In Memory of Sigmund Freud', 1939)

All points of view can be heard: . . . in endlessly dragging debates over the media, the stupid opinion is treated with the same respect as the intelligent one, the misinformed may talk as long as the informed, and propaganda rides along with education, truth with falsehood. This pure toleration of sense and nonsense is justified by the democratic argument that . . . all contesting opinions must be submitted to 'the people' for its deliberation and choice. . . . Other words can be spoken and heard, other ideas can be expressed, but, at the massive scale of the conservative majority (outside such enclaves as the intelligentsia), they are immediately 'evaluated' (i.e. automatically understood) in terms of the public language – a language which determines 'a priori' the direction in which the thought process moves.
(Herbert Marcuse, 'Repressive Tolerance')[19]

Fake and true
A few days after the electoral victory of Donald Trump, in an interview with the *Washington Post* Paul Horner, a professional fabricator of hoaxes, credited himself with being responsible for Trump's victory.

> My sites were picked up by Trump supporters all the time. I think Trump is in the White House because of me. His followers don't fact-check anything – they'll post everything, believe anything.[20]

Horner is the man behind such viral headlines as 'The Amish in America Commit their Vote to Donald Trump' and 'President Obama Signs Executive Order Banning the National Anthem at all Sporting Events Nationwide' – neither of which was true.

Trump's supporters were probably heartened in September 2016, when, according to an article shared nearly a million times on Facebook, the candidate received an endorsement from Pope Francis. And their opinion of Hillary Clinton is likely to have soured even further after reading a *Denver Guardian* article that also quickly spread on Facebook, which reported days before the election that an FBI agent suspected of involvement in leaking Mrs Clinton's emails was found dead in an apparent murder-suicide. There was just one problem with these articles: they were completely fake.[21]

Commentators, journalists and politicians have blamed the increasing unreliability of social media, denouncing the effects of false information on political life. Democratic commentators are appalled by the spread of fake news, and cling to the assumption that announcements and the like should be based on facts. However, it's hard to answer the question: what is a fact?

Before discovering that Facebook was routinely trading users' data to Cambridge Analytica and similar political and economic agencies, some people blamed Mark Zuckerberg for the role played by social media (particularly Facebook) in the electoral contest. However, it's not clear what Zuckerberg should do: censor the news and comments that don't correspond to truth?

What is truth? And who is to say what the difference is between false and true news, who's to judge what are legitimate and what illegitimate comments?

Kenan Malik in the *New York Times*:

> The panic about fake news has given fuel to the idea that we live in a 'post-truth era'. The *Oxford English Dictionary* has even made post-truth its 'word of the year' in 2016, defining it as 'circumstances in which objective facts are less influential in shaping public opinion than appeals to emotion and personal belief'. But the truth, if I may still use this word, is more complex than many allow.[22]

Furthermore, in his article Malik argues that truth is based on trustability, on the authority of sources, the gatekeepers of truth. What is crumbling in the Trump/age is the reliability of the sources of public discourse, the reliability of authority.

Hard to define the meaning of the word 'truth', as truth is not an attribute of the entity, but a subjective attribution. Of what?

How can we say when an enunciation is true?

The word 'parrhesia', debated by Foucault in his seminary, should not be translated as 'truth'; in fact it refers rather to ethical and political frankness, the freedom to say what one thinks.

According to Kant, the enunciations of language may be ranged as analytic and synthetic sentences. In the analytic sentence, the predicate is only a specification of the subject. In mathematical enunciations, for instance, the conclusion is a deployment of what is already in the premise.

The analytic truth is therefore a mere effect of logical coherence.

Synthetic sentences, on the other hand, are based on the permanent hiatus between subject and predicate. The hiatus is an interruption but also an opening. As an interruption, the hiatus breaks the chain of meaning; as an opening, it engenders the process of signification. The discourse of life aims not at truth, but at pragmatic effects, and meaning shifts from one level of interpretation to the next.

Outside the tautological sphere of mathematics, the notion of truth sounds empty, and there is no isomorphic relation between language and factual reality.

Verification or falsification is based not on factual correlation, but on pragmatic efficacy. The final criterion of truth is ethical, political and aesthetic, not ontological.

Fake, noise and shitstorm
In public discourse, there are enunciations that pretend to be factual while they are simulating

facts, and building interpretations on these simulations.

The Western political world has recently discovered the political effect of fake news (the simulation of pseudo-facts spreading across social communication), but the fabrication of the fake has been a constant feature of media communication throughout late modern times.

Think of modern advertising. It is a semiotic chain whose mission is to create simulated expectations, so as to lure people into consumption, life choices, ideological mind frames.

Advertising is the ubiquitous flow of fake information that systematically models expectations, imagination, subconscious life.

So fake news is everywhere in the mass media age and has always influenced political choices.

The claim that nationalism is winning because of fake news does not persuade me. I rather think that the cause of the current shift towards nationalism and fascism is to be found in the failure of democracy in the age of neoliberal governance. Democracy has proven impotent in countering financial predation, so impoverished workers are trying another way, and the only way that is left is fascism. For an expanding part of the Western population the point is not truth, but revenge. Trump is disgusting? Yes, he is disgusting, and this is why well-mannered, centre-left politicians despise him – and this is why white working people have voted for him.

The fanatical propagators of conspiracy theories, fake news and racist, anti-feminist aggression proclaim that they represent American freedom of speech. They are right, but the problem is the content of their freedom.

In theocratic times, truth used to be identified with the utterance of power, coming from God. Power was the source of reason and of law, and the voice of power commanded the multitude's silence.

Lately, power is no longer synonymous with reason and law. Power no longer commands silence. On the contrary, power is now the master of noise. The exercise of power is based on simulation and nervous hyper-stimulation.

The new discursive weapon of power is the shitstorm. The shitstorm redefines the very source of power. In the book *In the Swarm*, the Korean-German philosopher Byung-Chul Han says that:

> Shit-storms occur for many reasons. They arise in a culture where respect is lacking and indiscretion prevails. The shit-storm represents an authentic phenomenon of digital communication.[23]

What Byung-Chul Han calls 'shit-storm' may be defined as the mutation of the public discourse into war among a-signifiers. In the semiotic dimension that we may label 'shitstorm', the goal of semiotic emission (the intention of the participants in the chat) is not to produce meaning, but to compete and to win. The enunciation is nothing but a weapon. 'Unlike the crowd, the swarm demonstrates no internal coherence. It does not speak with a *voice*. The shit-storm lacks a *voice*, too. Accordingly, it is perceived as *noise*.'[24]

The very foundation of political power is reframed in the hyper-saturated infosphere. No longer is it ideological consensus or dogmatic obedience that is the foundation of power, but noise, mental confusion, discharge of emotional distress, and revenge for humiliation.

> Sovereignty needs to be redefined in light of shit-storms. According to Carl Schmitt, sovereignty is a matter of deciding when a state of exception

holds. This doctrine may be translated into acoustic terms. Sovereignty means being able to produce *absolute quiet* – eliminating all noise and making all others fall silent in a single stroke. . . . In light of electromagnetic waves, he even found it necessary to reformulate his famous thesis on sovereignty: 'After the First World War, I said: "Sovereign is he who decides on the exception." After the Second World War . . . I now say: "Sovereign is he who commands the waves of space." . . . Following the digital revolution, we need to reformulate Schmitt's words on sovereignty yet again: *Sovereign is he who commands the shitstorms of the Net.*[25]

Extinction of the critical mind

I don't deny that the volume of false information is expanding in political discourse, nor do I deny that it is detrimental to democracy and useful for the bad guys. But false information is nothing new in public discourse.

Journalists and politicians express their indignation because Russian hackers are influencing elections in democratic Western countries. This is bad but hardly new, as in the last seventy years the American media system and the American secret services have systematically influenced elections in many countries, not only in the West but almost everywhere.

American money influenced the Italian general election in the year 1948, and the American secret service influenced the fall of Mohammad Mosaddegh in Iraq in 1953, just to name two examples. And the American media have played a clear role in pushing people to rebel (with good reason, of course) during the anti-Soviet demonstrations of 1989 and the Ukrainian insurrection of 2014.

So nothing new in fake news.

What is new is the speed and intensity of info-stimulation, and therefore the enormous amount of attention that is absorbed by information (fake or otherwise).

This saturation of social attention is jeopardizing our critical skills.

Critical skills are not a natural given, but a product of intellectual evolution through history. The cognitive faculty we call 'critique' is the individual's ability to distinguish between true and false statements, as well as the ability to distinguish between good and evil acts, and it only develops under special conditions. In fact, in order to distinguish critically, our mind needs to process information, then consider, then decide. Criticality implies a rhythmic relation between information stimulus and elaboration time.

Beyond a certain level of intensity, information is no longer received and interpreted as a complex set of statements. Rather it is perceived as a flow of nervous stimulations, an emotional assault on the brain.

The critical faculty that was crucial in the formation of public opinion in the modern bourgeois age was the effect of a special relationship between the individual mind and the infosphere, particularly the sphere consisting of printed media, books and public discussion.

The alphabetical mind was engaged to elaborate a slow flux of words sequentially disposed on the page, so public discourse was a space of conscious evaluation and critical discrimination, and political choice was based on critical assessment and ideological discernment.

The acceleration of info-flows led to the saturation of attention, so that our ability to discriminate between what is true and what is false becomes confused, and disturbed; the storm of info-stimulation blurs the vision, and people come to wrap themselves up in networks of self-confirmation.

Twenty-five years ago, our imagination of the emerging internet was based on the idea that this new dimension was destined to break down all the borders and enable a process of broad and free confrontation.

But we were only partially right: the internet has turned into a space where countless echo chambers reverberate, always repeating the same message: competition, identity, aggressiveness.

As far as I can understand, the main problem of the contemporary mediascape is not the spread of fake news, but the decomposition of the critical mind, with effects that include gullibility amongst large crowds and the self-confirming aggressiveness of the multitude.

In the above-mentioned interview with the *Washington Post*, Horner offers the following explanation of the affirmation of Trump: 'Honestly, people are definitely dumber. They just keep passing stuff around. Nobody fact-checks anything anymore – I mean, that's how Trump got elected.'[26]

The cultural regression of our time is not rooted in the increased number of lies circulating in the infosphere. It is rather an effect of the inability of the social mind to elaborate critical distinctions, the inability of people to prioritize their own social experience and create a common pathway for autonomous subjectivation. This is why people vote for media-manipulators who in turn exploit their gullibility.

In the European Union, there is much talk about passing regulations against fake news. Who will decide the limits between false and true?

Should we fight for the re-establishment of truth in order to restore democracy?

The fight to unmask the official media's lies has always been an essential point on the agenda of social movements, but I don't think that the main task of the social movement is the fight for truth.

Despite the complications of public discourse and the uncountable lies that circulate in politicians' talk, it is not so difficult to know the truth, and most people are well aware of what is true: we learn by experience that capitalism is exploiting our work, and that financial dynamics is impoverishing society. After two decades of neoliberal bamboozlement, an increasing number of people have come to realize that capitalism is a trap. What we don't know is how to get out of the trap. We don't know how to reactivate the social body's autonomy. We don't need someone who denounces the reality of exploitation; we need someone who tells us how to get rid of exploitation.

This is why I have mixed feelings when it comes to the extraordinary adventure of WikiLeaks. When WikiLeaks revealed that the American army had killed unarmed civilians in Afghanistan and elsewhere, it did a useful job for the world of journalism, but did not add much to what we already know. Almost everybody knows that the hyper-modern military routinely kill innocent people. Only 9 per cent of the victims in World War I were civilians. In the wars fought at the end of the twentieth century, more than 90 per cent of the victims were civilians.

In itself, being informed of predation and violence does not help people to organize and to get free from the grip of power. It may rather be disheartening.

Not the truth but the imagination of lines of escape helps people to live an autonomous life, and to rebel successfully.

I think that Julian Assange has done a great job

in enhancing the power of independent information, but his contribution to the movement of emancipation does not consist in revealing the truth. What is more interesting for me is another, less visible side: WikiLeaks has been an important experience of solidarity among journalists, computer scientists and military personnel who rebelled against the hypocrisy and the inhumanity of war. This is the invaluable merit of WikiLeaks and other hacktivist actors.

But the obsession with truth that belongs to the Puritanical culture has produced ambiguous effects, to the point where some revelations have played into the hands of Trump and of Putin.

The philosophy of WikiLeaks is based on the description of power in terms of secrecy: secrets are seen as the source of authority and of command.

If one discloses the secret, the truth can be established.

But the truth is ineffective in itself, because the game of enunciation is an infinite one. Once you discover the secret content, you face the riddle of interpretation. Interpretation is the ultimate decider and the enabler of action, and interpretation is an infinite game that can only be decided by an act of will and also by an act of aesthetic inclination.

Rather than being secret, the signs of power are enigmatic.

The source of power is enigma: we never cease to look for authentication, and we don't find it because power has no authenticity.

The secret is a content hidden from public view. You need the key that enables you to open the safe and you will know the hidden truth.

However, the process of social subjectivation is not based on disclosing the secret; it is based on the process of interpretation, and imagination.

The enigma is an open enunciation that may be interpreted in infinite ways, and the enunciations of power are much more similar to enigmas than to secrets. You have to continuously interpret the signs of established power in order to find lines of escape and lines of subjectivation.

The conflict between WikiLeaks and the Western establishment develops inside the Anglo-Saxon sphere of Puritanism. As Jonathan Franzen grasped quite sharply in *Purity*, digital culture is the point of arrival of the epistemological binarization and purification of language and of social behaviour.[27]

What we have here is a conflict between two different forms of Puritanical culture: the centre-left cult of political correctness versus the WikiLeaks cult of an ethical truth that political correctness often hypocritically masks.

But at the end of the contest, the winner was the Trump baroque: the Emperor of Fake rising from the ruins of social solidarity and of critical understating.

Chaos wins against order, and artificial noise wins against human voices.

Auschwitz on the Beach

August 2016: every day thousands of people from Syria, Afghanistan, Nigeria, Sudan and other countries where life is dangerous because of wars, hunger, environmental devastation were trying to find refuge on the European continent. From the East they tried the Balkan route and were rejected at the Hungarian border; from the South they tried to traverse the Mediterranean Sea and risked shipwreck and death.

They were systematically rejected by the authorities of European countries, and by the majority of the European population. August

2016 is a turning point: since then, humanitarian sentiments have been overcome by fear and resentment.

Since August 2016, millions of persons who are escaping wars, hunger, environmental disaster have been rejected by the majority of European countries, with the exception of Greece and Italy, the poorest countries of the Union, willy-nilly (more nilly than willy) obliged to receive those who manage to disembark or those who were rescued by NGOs.

The more migrants drown in the sea, the more pictures of wrecked boats are published in newspapers, the more Europeans turn hostile to migration. Anguish and concern prevail over compassion, and racism grows, mixed with self-loathing and rage. The European malaise has found a scapegoat, a victim that can easily be aggressed.

The German government, which in 2015 had opened the door to one million migrants, was hit by a wave of popular discontent, so powerful and massive that Angela Merkel was obliged to backpedal and to sign an agreement with the Turkish strongman in order to stop the migrant wave from the Middle East (particularly from

Syria). The great migration, expected since the 1990s, was approaching a peak, and the European population, impoverished by ten years of financial plundering and infuriated by political impotence, refused to accept the toll of migration, and to take responsibility for the consequences of two hundred years of colonialism.

Since summer 2016, restrictive measures have been enforced by the countries of Europe. Fences and walls have been built. All around the Mediterranean coast, concentration camps have been mushrooming, from Leros to Lesbos, from Moria to Idomeni, from Lampedusa to Calais to Ventimiglia to Ceuta and so on.

Migrants are seen by the majority of Europeans as a danger; nevertheless, they are welcome as slaves in the southern Italian plantations or in sweatshops all over the continent.

Three thousand migrants are officially said to have drowned in the Mediterranean Sea in 2016, more in 2017. Many more are dying in the camps of Libya.

In those days of summer 2016 I wrote a poem, titled 'Auschwitz on the Beach', and I spoke with my brother, a musician, and with an artist whose name is Dim Sampajo, and together we imagined a performance for the art exhibition documenta 14, held in Kassel, Germany and in Athens in 2017.

My brother wrote three minutes of music mixing marimba melody and a Philip Glass loop in a distressing rhythm. Dim imagined the visual stage of the performance: a square of salt six metres by six metres, glimmering in the light of a big lamp. All around, darkness.

The performance has never been staged, and the poem no longer exists, as I deleted the text from my computer.

I'll shortly explain why.

No-performance

The performance was scheduled for 24 August 2017, 8pm, in the Fridericianum building in Kassel. Just a few days before, I received some messages from the press office of documenta 14, then a phone call from Paul Preciado, its public service director. The German press was launching a campaign to denounce the title of the performance as a 'relativization of the Holocaust'.

Not the performance, but the title.

Mentioning Auschwitz in the frivolous context of the beach raised sentiments of disgust, of guilt and rejection among righteous journalists and their readers. Obviously I had been expecting a reaction since that title first came into my imagination, reverberating with Robert Wilson and Philip Glass's *Einstein on the Beach*. I had been expecting a reaction to the intentionally provocative title, but the reaction that I got was much larger and harsher than expected: the political authorities of the *Land*, some Jewish cultural centres, and the whole of the national press accused me of relativization of the Shoah.

When I received a second call from Paul Preciado, and noticed a certain understandable anxiety in his voice, I plainly told him: 'Let's cancel the performance.'

Some friends think that I bent to an act of censorship. It is not true.

When I realized that the performance was under attack, I focused on the message that I intended to spread, not on my freedom of expression.

And the message is: beware. What the Europeans are doing in the Mediterranean will be a permanent stain for generations to come. This stain will mark European peoples as the Holocaust marks German historical memory.

Here it is not my freedom of expression that

is at stake, but the lives of millions of women and men that European cynicism is exposing to extreme danger. Therefore I willingly renounce my freedom of speech, if I can call attention to the infamy that is under way.

Having cancelled the performance, we called for a talk in the Rotunda of the Fridericianum, and we named the event 'Shame on Us'.

The first thing I did as soon as I arrived in Kassel was to go to the Sara Nussbaum Centre, the main Jewish cultural centre in the town.

We sat around a long rectangular table: six representatives of the centre, me, Paul Preciado and Adam Smetzjek, the Polish curator who co-directed documenta 14. The discussion was extremely meaningful, and friendly. A samovar was at the centre of the table.

'I know that you were not motivated by anti-Semitic intentions', said Eva Schulz-Jander, coordinator of the Gesellschaften für Christlich–Jüdische Zusammenarbeit (Organizations for Christian–Jewish Cooperation); then she reminded us that in 1938, German Jews trying to migrate to the United Kingdom and to the United States experienced the same rejection as today's migrants, with similar motivations.

Numbers of those Jews eventually died in the Nazis' concentration camps.

I said that the intention of our performance was to use Auschwitz as a shield, as a protection against the danger of a return of Auschwitz.

The meeting closed, and we left the room in friendship, promising each other to stay in contact. Paul and Adam invited the members of the Sara Nussbaum Centre to come to the evening event, 'Shame on Us'. Three of them actually came, and their presence during the discussion was overwhelmingly important, even crucial.

At 8.30 the Rotunda was crowded. You can see the video-recording at this link: http://www.documenta14.de/en/calendar/24356/shame-on-us-a-reading-and-discussion.

My talk was about the current extermination.

I gave some information: the official figure for how many people have died in the Mediterranean only during the current year: 3,000. How many are possibly dead according to unofficial figures. How many people are dying in the deserts because of the blocks the European governments have put in place. After giving some information of this kind, I reclaimed the right to define the measures of rejection by the name 'extermination'. I remarked that the process is only starting.

I went on to say that the European population is starting a war, a war against migration, as George W. Bush started a war in 2003. And this war we will lose, as the Americans have lost their wars in Afghanistan and Iraq. The white people will lose their wars for two simple reasons.

The first reason is that, thanks to the deregulation of the market, weapons of mass destruction are no longer a prerogative of white Westerners.

Kim Jong-un has recently declared that Western people have to wake up from their dream that death concerns only others. Now, in the words of Kim, 'We are able to bring death into your lands.'

This is technically true: nuclear technology has escaped the control of the white potentates of the world.

Secondly, since bin Laden wreaked havoc in Manhattan and unleashed a war that the US has lost, an army of suicidal avengers is periodically terrorizing European cities, and will not stop doing so.

The army of potential avengers is immense.

Only peace, solidarity, open arms and the

redistribution of wealth are the way to escape a war that we are already losing, a war that will destroy the daily life of our cities and of our children.

This is what I said in my talk.

The following days the attitude of the press changed, partially.

Some journalists distanced themselves from the prevailing discourse. Philipp Ruch, in the *Süddeutsche Zeitung*, observed that yes, maybe the title 'Auschwitz on the Beach' is a little bit brutal, but the concentration camps in Libya and elsewhere are brutal too.

3

Is There Life after the Apocalypse?

Enlightenment is not only a state, but an event, and a process. As the designation for an historical episode, concentrated in northern Europe during the 18th century, it is a leading candidate for the 'true name' of modernity, capturing its origin and essence. Between 'enlightenment' and 'progressive enlightenment' there is only an elusive difference, because illumination takes time – and feeds on itself, because enlightenment is self-confirming, its revelations 'self evident', and because a retrograde, or reactionary, 'dark enlightenment' amounts almost to intrinsic contradiction. To become enlightened, in this historical sense, is to recognize, and then to pursue, a guiding light. (Land, 'Dark Enlightenment').[1]

IS THERE LIFE AFTER THE APOCALYPSE?

Dark Enlightenment: The End of Critical Reason

'Dark Enlightenment' is the expression that defines a neo-reactionary tendency influential in the alt-right movement in the US and generally in the West. The Western neo-reactionary tendency can be only partially assimilated to Duginism, the theory elaborated by the Russian thinker Akexander Dugin, inasmuch as American neo-reactionaries build on the libertarian cult for deregulation and aim at the final dissolution of the state, while Russian neo-reactionaries consider the sovereign state as the condition for the establishment of a new Euro-Asian order.

Nevertheless, those two tendencies have much in common, as they want to replace democracy, which is based on critical opinion with the identitarian culture of belonging.

As Duginism has been influential in the emergence of Putin's authoritarianism and in the project of re-establishing national sovereignty in many European countries, the political implications of the alt-right movement have become evident in recent years with the victory of Trump: his ideological adviser Steve Bannon, half-ironically defining himself a Leninist, declared that destroying the state is the main goal of the movement represented by the new president of the US.

Democratic liberalism has been the hegemonic ideological framework of late modern history, but since the end of the twentieth century the libertarian version of liberal capitalism (linked to the social Darwinist version of digital culture) has eroded the ground of democracy to the point where now the utter dismissal of democracy is under way.

Neoliberal hyper-capitalism has finally resulted in the resurrection of Nazism.

> Democracy and 'progressive democracy' are synonymous, and indistinguishable from the expansion of the state. Whilst 'extreme right wing' governments have, on rare occasions, momentarily arrested this process, its reversal lies beyond the bounds of democratic possibility. Since winning elections is overwhelmingly a matter of vote buying, and society's informational organs (education and media) are no more resistant to bribery than the electorate, a thrifty politician is simply an incompetent politician, and the democratic variant of Darwinism

quickly eliminates such misfits from the gene pool. This is a reality that the left applauds, the establishment right grumpily accepts, and the libertarian right has ineffectively railed against. Increasingly, however, libertarians have ceased to care whether anyone is 'pay[ing them] attention' – they have been looking for something else entirely: an exit.[2]

György Lukács defined Nazism as the destruction of reason: this destruction is happening again. Why do an increasing number of Western people want, for the second time, to destroy reason? Rationality is not a natural given, and reason does not correspond to a natural setting of thought. Critical reason is a result of an anthropological disposition and of a technical organization of public discourse. Jack Goody argues that logical thinking is based on the availability of written lists and readable texts,[3] and Michel Foucault has described the creation of the modern kingdom of reason from the perspective of the marginalization and eventual segregation of unreason.[4] Unreason was expelled from the social scene so that critical reasoning could become the hegemonic form of cognition and the condition for the political regulation of social life.

Alphabetical technology and printed transmission of texts were the precondition of the critical elaboration that enabled the political experiment of liberal democracy.

Then, following the spread of electronic and digital technology, the acceleration of the infosphere provoked the explosion of the critical and rational organization of the contents of public discourse: this is currently why we have the legitimate impression that madness is spreading everywhere in the social domain.

Furthermore, after 2008, financial domination, embodied in the enforcing of debt as the only rational management of the economy, has led a large part of the Euro-American population to identify reason with the financial algorithm. At this point, modern reason has come to be perceived as an enemy of life.

Dark Enlightenment is an effective way to define the actual darkening of the social mind, but it is also the ironic recognition of the impending decay of human rationality.

The surge of the neo-reactionary wave all over the world is not, in my humble opinion, an essentially political event: it is much more understandable as the epiphenomenon of an anthropological mutation. Therefore I don't expect that the present involution will be reversed by the democratic vote or by some kind of political action: it is not a political effect, so it cannot be politically overcome.

I think, on the contrary, that the wave of racist and nationalist aggressiveness is destined to feed on itself: this is why I call it apocalyptic. The question now is the following: will the human mind imagine a human, post-apocalyptic form of life? Will a new idea of humanism emerge from the wreckage of humanism?

I don't have an answer. The only thing we can do is to create a meme for the post-apocalyptic era.

The Second Coming of Hitler

In my childhood, my father told me a million times: 'You are lucky because you'll never see fascism again, you'll never see war again.'

Lucky for him that he died before seeing his prediction was wrong.

Now the question is: will war end one day? Will fascism be defeated again? Is there a way out?

IS THERE LIFE AFTER THE APOCALYPSE?

In the past, politics was the dimension of the fight against oppression. No longer so, because today politics has lost its potency; because the hyper-complexity of the socio-media sphere has bypassed the processing power of the rational mind; and because conscious volition has lost its ability to govern both the flows of social unconsciousness that are spreading chaotically, and the inexorability of the networked automaton.

Far from being immutable, the past, which only exists in our memory, is continuously changing, as we discover new facets that were previously unknown. So the meaning of the twentieth century has changed in our perception during the last fifteen years. Little by little, we have been led to see the events of the past in a different light, in a sort of retrospective dystopia, as a nightmare that comes back in daylight.

In the new light of the Trump/age, sometimes I have the creepy feeling that the victory of democracy over Hitler has been a sort of *trompe l'oeil*.

Although it failed in the 1940s thanks to the sacrifice of some 25 million Soviet citizens, to the organized resistance of partisans and to the American air force, Nazism may be viewed today as an experiment that is now coming back, in a different light and with different colours, and with expanded magnitude.

In the last few years, we have learned the hard way that capitalism and democracy are incompatible: after decades of social conflict within the democratic framework, impelled by the dynamics of global competition, capitalism finally lost its flexibility, and, neglecting the promise of democracy, entered into the abstract dimension of financial automatism. The inflexibility of the financial constriction has deactivated democracy and pushed political reason into impotence. And impotence, in turn, has provoked the reawakening of racism and national aggressiveness. Now it seems too late for a political recovery and a peaceful outcome: depression and social precariousness have eroded the roots of social autonomy, social democracy is defeated everywhere, and the worldwide extension of right-wing revengeful aggression looks like the promise of long-lasting destruction and war.

Unlike the Italian brand of fascism, which was based on the traditional features of homely oppression (sexual, familiar, agricultural), Nazism was marked by the *unheimlich* vibrations of a non-human violence.

IS THERE LIFE AFTER THE APOCALYPSE?

Italian fascism was the clownish exhibition of masculine force, the spectacular excess of baroque inessentiality. Nazism was based instead on the Gothic aptness for severity and technical strictness, and contempt for the inessential.

The postmodern Leviathan combines the baroque stimulation overload that is typical of the electronic media system with the Gothic perfection of digital connectivity.

According to Günther Anders, the central feature of Nazism is automated inhumanity. While Italian fascism was essentially based on the face-to-face relation of humiliation, violence and submission, in the Nazi sphere human beings were no longer needed to humiliate and to murder: Auschwitz was an industrialized machine for extermination.

'Hier ist kein warum', writes Primo Levi in *Se questo è un uomo*.[5] No reasons: functionality alone is the point of the hellish order of the Auschwitz machine.

Anders considered Nazism as the anticipation of the 'Reich to come'.

Is the Reich to come finally here? Financial violence does not need men to humiliate and to murder; the financial machine automatically does its job: mathematical perfection is not reasonable, is not pretending to be moral, or politically correct. It works, it's operative, it is performing its task, and that is that.

After spending ten unforgettable summers on the island of Ischia, W. H. Auden wrote somewhere that although we cannot always remember the reason why, nevertheless we cannot forget that we have been happy.[6] I know that happiness is possible and that friendship is possible, and solidarity, which is the contagious dimension of friendship, is possible too, even if it's difficult to remember exactly why and how. Now it is difficult even to imagine solidarity, not to mention happiness. Now the talk is about surviving homelessness and unemployment, war and extermination: how can we think of friendship and of happiness when survival itself is at stake, and particularly when the prospect of survival is based on all-pervading competition, on all-pervading war?

The Congress of Versailles was the first global event in the history of the world. June 1919: all the nations, with the remarkable exception of Soviet Russia, convened in Paris, and in the royal palace of Versailles spent six months talking about everything. During the event, those who had won the First World War tried to shape the world to suit their convenience.

For the first time in history, a general agreement about the map of the world was attempted in the spirit of self-determination outlined by Woodrow Wilson.

However, those who had lost the war, particularly the Germans but also the Italians – formally winners, substantially losers – entered on a cycle of humiliation and revenge.

The year 1919 can be recorded as the moment in which the political landscape of modernity came to be fully shaped and fully perceived as a world-scape.

In the same year, William Butler Yeats wrote *The Second Coming*.

It is a text about the collapse of social order, the decomposition of civilization:

> Things fall apart; the centre cannot hold;
> Mere anarchy is loosed upon the world,
> The blood-dimmed tide is loosed, and everywhere
> The ceremony of innocence is drowned;
> The best lack all conviction, while the worst
> Are full of passionate intensity.

IS THERE LIFE AFTER THE APOCALYPSE?

In the years following the immense devastation of the First World War, Yeats speaks of the painful, blood-dimmed chaos that is loosed upon the world, and he sees signs of the second coming of Jesus Christ:

Surely the second coming is at hand.

The second coming of Jesus Christ was Yeats' expectation.

However, in the decade after 1919, Jesus Christ did not come.

Hitler did.

Now an apocalyptic model seems the best suited for describing the surrounding landscape, from many points of view. Let's not forget that the apocalypse is an event that reveals the hidden rationale of the cosmos: chaos. But the apocalypse is also the moment in which a hidden possibility comes to be revealed. If we are unable to see and to actualize the hidden possibility, the descent into nothing will follow.

Have we already lost the opportunity of actualizing the possibility, or is the possibility still alive?

Is the human mind ossified and ruled by the

cognitive automaton, or is conscious subjectivity latent and still able to reorganize?

The Communist Meme

I read Yeats' text from the perspective of today, and I want to interpret his words in a non-theological way: my second coming has a worldly sound. I'm trying to imagine how to break the spell of impotence and despair that overshadows the psychosphere of our time, and how to reinvent a future beyond the impending apocalypse and the trauma it is going to bring about. I call this prospect (no matter how unrealistic it may sound) the second coming of Communism.

I know that the word 'Communism' has lost credibility because of the historical experience of authoritarian Communist states. I know that we need better words to define the possibility that is inscribed in the present. Nevertheless, I pronounce this word as a sign of contempt for intellectual cynicism, and as a sign of respect for the proletarians who died fighting against exploitation. Communism means getting rid of the superstition of accumulation and of salaried work: it means egalitarianism and emancipation of social time. These possibilities are at hand thanks to the connective general intellect, but the social mind is unable to actualize this possibility, because the social mind is subjected to the force of replication of the dominant memes.

I use the word 'Communism' as a provisional conceptual tool, but I'm not referring to any ideological vision, to any systematic project of transformation, or to any political programme for the government of the future. None of these.

I am thinking of the creation of memes for disentanglement.

In the relation between knowledge technology and labour, a conundrum is contained: thanks to techno-automation, less and less labour time is necessary, but this is releasing a wave of fear, misery and violence. How is such a paradox possible?

This paradox is based on the superstition of salary. We have been accustomed to think that our survival is only possible if we exchange our time for money. We have been led to think that salaried labour is a natural law.

It is not: it is a convention based on a *rapport de force* between owners and proletarians, between exploiters and exploited. The consumerist memes and the memes of competition reinforce the superstition.

The way out of the labyrinth is emancipation from the superstition of salaried labour, and I'm calling this emancipation 'Communism': memes provoking a reset of our expectations. In my parlance, the word 'Communism' is the trigger for a process of memetic disentanglement of the possibility that is inscribed in the network of the general intellect.

When I say 'Communism', I use this word to refer to the meme that has to be created, engineered and set in motion on the post-apocalyptic scene.

A meme is a unit of signification that is embodied in a sign, in a word, in an image, in a gesture. A meme has to be easily replicated and memorized: it must also be a mneme (unit of memorization).

In an article titled 'They Say We Can't Meme: Politics of Idea Compression', Geert Lovink and Marc Tuters write:

> memes [are] one of many ways to understand the fast and dark world of the mindset of today's online subject. We see memes as densely com-

pressed, open contradictions, designed to circulate in our real-time networks that work with repeating elements. As the far-right have discovered, memes express tensions that can't be spoken in the political [*sic*] correct vocabulary of the mainstream media. To what extent can these empty formats symbolize the lived experience of global capitalism? Is it true that the left can't meme? These are the strategic questions faced by activists and social media campaigners today.[7]

The proliferation of memes in the mind-scape of our time is an effect of the transition from the alphabetical to the immersive infosphere.

In *Understanding Media* (1964), Marshall McLuhan stated that as the media system shifts from the printed alphabetical technology of communication to the electronic networked one, mental elaboration moves from the mode of sequentiality to the mode of simultaneity.[8]

This implies that critical reason, which was able to sequentially discriminate the true from the false in public discourse, has given way to a comeback of mythological thought, which is no longer able to discriminate and is surfing on waves of nervous stimulation.

This is why, in the public discourse of our time, ideological criticality is replaced by the contagion of memes.

Lovink and Tuters remark that the meme-oriented mind-scape favours the politics of the right wing, and suggest that 'the left can't meme'.

> Memes, however, are merely cultural bi-products [*sic*] of the app ecosystem; the medium, not the meme, is the message. Memes are eyewash of an optimization arms race that strives to reach as far down into the limbic system as possible.

Here is the point: can Communism re-emerge as a memetic short circuit in the impending mental chaos? Will we be able to transform the rational prospect of disentanglement from the superstition of salaried labour, and the actualization of the possibility inscribed in the networked potency of the general intellect, into memetic messages and memetic gestures?

In the crystal ball of this century, I see the expansion of chaos and the simultaneous concatenation of the automaton. This double trend seems unavoidable. Nevertheless, we should never forget that the unavoidable generally does not happen, because the unpredictable prevails at the end of the day, as Maynard Keynes is said to have written somewhere.

Our first task is to describe the unavoidable: look straight into the eyes of the beast. Simultaneously, however, we have to remember that game-changing events are unpredictable. So our second task is to be intellectually ready for the game change.

The more complex the system grows, the less we can predict the effects of a marginal cultural trend, of an unknown technical discovery. Therefore, despair notwithstanding, we should not stop exercising the art of thinking and the art of philosophical imagination.

I know that thought is dismissed as so much old ballast in the age of communication and speed. Thought seems ineffective and ornamental, I know. But this is part of the unavoidable, and my concern is the unpredictable.

Don't stop thinking, because the unpredictable may soon need some thought, and this is our job: thinking in times of apocalyptic trauma.

The Illusion of Privacy and the Reality of Cognitive Automation

The divergence (and the interplay) of the old printed media and the new immersive media has hastened to the point of dramatically marking the political history of the world. The victory of Trump in the US, the worldwide triumph of nationalism, and the crisis (not, however, the collapse) of neoliberal globalization have been blamed as the effects of a sort of gigantic manipulation of public opinion by global agencies intentionally engaged in the dissemination of fake news. The role of Facebook has been especially emphasized, when the *Guardian* and the *New York Times* divulged that Cambridge Analytica, an agency involved in the electoral campaign of Donald Trump, had gained access to millions of Facebook profiles. Well-intentioned liberals and the democratic printed press have launched a worldwide campaign aimed at fixing Facebook and finally submitting the global media companies to the rule of democracy and reason.

In April 2018, the US Congress summoned Mark Zuckerberg, trying to find a way to rein in Facebook and, first of all, trying to understand what the link is between social networks and the dynamics that is breaking the very machinery of democracy. In a column published in the *New York Times*, Kevin Roose wrote that Congress has the power to fix Facebook and to restore the rule of democracy in the field of media.

> The biggest obstacle to regulating Facebook is not Congress's lack of computer literacy . . . It's a lack of political will, and an unwillingness to identify the problems they're trying to fix.[9]

Is this true? I don't think so.

The biggest obstacle is that the rationale of the global semiotic agencies escapes the rationale and the scope of law and political government. What is the problem with Facebook, and Google, and Apple, just to name the biggest semio-companies?

> Is it that Facebook is too cavalier about sharing user data with outside organizations?
>
> Is it that Facebook collects too much data about users in the first place?
>
> Is it that Facebook is promoting addictive messaging products to children?

Is it that Facebook's news feed is polarizing society, pushing people to ideological fringes?

Is it that Facebook is too easy for political operatives to exploit, or that it does not do enough to keep false news and hate speech off users' feeds?

Is it that Facebook is simply too big, or a monopoly that needs to be broken up?[10]

I think that none of these questions gets the point. The point is that Facebook, and the connective immersive media in general, have already and for good obliterated the very possibility of critical understanding, of political decision, and (most troubling) Facebook has put in motion a process of automated simulation of social relations like friendship, while Google has put in motion a process of automated simulation of cognition at large.

This process of cognitive automation is intrinsic to the technical nature of connective forms of interaction, not the effect of malignant political intentions, and therefore it is irreversible, and happens at a level that political will and decision cannot touch. The dimension in which political rule can act (national territory, rational and critical understanding) does not coincide with the dimension of connective immersion, which is deterritorialized and non-complying with political will and with critical reason.

The well-intentioned journalists of the *New York Times* represent the globalist liberal culture that has ruled Western countries throughout the late modern decades. Those who have ruled the economy since the days of Thatcher, then of Blair, cannot accept the idea that Trump is trumping the world. So the pundits look for an explanation for the unconscionable defeat suffered by neoliberal governments almost everywhere, and find that the reverse has been caused by improper use of the media, manipulation of big data, and dissemination of fake news.

The truth, however, is much simpler: people have understood that the neoliberal elite, mostly centre-left, has surrendered social welfare in order to favour globalization and corporate profit. Those who used to vote for the left and for the centre are now prone to vote for the right-wing avengers. They understand that the Trumpists are going to destroy order, peace and progress, or at least they have a feeling that this is the likely future, but they despise the betrayers of the left to the point where they are ready to face chaos in order to punish them.

According to the liberal vision well expressed by the *New York Times*, our privacy is besieged and jeopardized by the media companies that sell data to advertising companies and to political agencies often linked to the right wing. This is true, of course. Since the rise of the social networks, the loss of privacy has been predictable and predicted, but people are willingly trading privacy in exchange for access to information, services, online shopping. Only naïve, self-deluding libertarians think that online transparency can come without total control. The problem is that privacy is not the main concern of many of the world's population, and attacks on our privacy and on our attention have been constant and ubiquitous since the beginning of media advertising, with or without Facebook and Google. The problem is that most people don't give a damn about the protection of their privacy because they have nothing to hide and to protect.

In the long run, the accumulation of data concerning our lifestyles, our preferences and our activities has created the conditions for the automation of everything.

Pope of Depression and Pope of Compassion

The best lack all conviction, says Yeats.

Think back to the former pope, the old German pope who came to Rome promising the final establishment of the truth: Benedict, otherwise Joseph Aloisius Ratzinger.

Ratzinger was an intellectual and a convinced supporter of absolute truth, and right-wing Catholics felt emboldened by his ascent to the throne. He said: 'God is one, and the Truth is one.'

In his best-known speech, delivered in Regensburg in 2006, the philosopher Ratzinger preached against relativism, which he regarded as the plague of modernity.

I'm not a fan of Nanni Moretti, generally, but I like *Habemus Papam*, the film that he directed in 2011, because it is a film about the fragility of human beings, including a human being who happens to be the pope. In the film, Michel Piccoli is elected pope; then, when he is expected to give his first public speech to the crowd assembled in St Peter's Square, he understands that he has nothing to say. All of a sudden he is overwhelmed by the reality of the world, mumbles 'I cannot speak', and he goes to see a psychoanalyst (who is, by the way, played by Nanni Moretti himself).

Pope Michel Piccoli is depressed, he is abruptly seeing the truth that he was trying to conceal: that there is no truth in the world.

In February 2013, Joseph Ratzinger decided to follow in the steps of Michel Piccoli.

These days, the relation between reality and imagination is growing more complicated than Jean Baudrillard could ever have imagined: the real pope imitates the actor impersonating the pope, and accepts the dark truth that he is not strong enough to sustain the responsibility of telling the truth because he feels that the truth is evading him.

Obviously, this is only my interpretation of Ratzinger's resignation, which in itself was an act of intellectual courage and moral humility. However, how can I interpret the decision of a pope who has been chosen by the Holy Spirit, and decides to resign against the will expressed by God himself, through the intermediation of the Holy Spirit? I think that the only possible interpretation is that Benedict felt his depression, and sincerely spoke with his God, and humbly revealed his intimate apocalypse.

Depression is neither a fault nor a limitation of the reasoning mind. It is the disconnection of reasoning from desire.

Then Mario Bergoglio was elected by the Consistory and he became the first Francis in the history of the popes. He went to the window and he said in effect: 'Buonasera. Good evening, I'm the man who comes from the end of the world', and he meant Argentina, a country ravaged by the beast of financial capitalism.

Since that moment, the apocalypse has been shining through Bergoglio's acts, because he is the man who dares to face the end.

From the end of the world, Francis has been opening a new path in theology.

Shortly after the election, he gave an interview published by the magazine *La Civiltà Cattolica*. The interview dwells on the three theological virtues: faith, hope and charity.

Obviously this is only my personal and philosophical interpretation of his words, but this is what I understand from Bergoglio's words. The main problem for Christians is not faith, today. Not Truth is the present problem of the church. Maybe tomorrow, who knows, but at the moment faith is not our focus. And if truth is put aside inoperative, then it is also difficult to have hope. Hope for the Christian is based on trust in God, and therefore on faith.

So no faith and no hope. Something is more urgent: our focus today has to be put on charity, on mercy, on the living existence of Jesus. He is not calling Christians to convert but to heal. The church, according to Bergoglio, has to be considered as a war hospital.

You may call it compassion, empathy among sentient beings. You may call it solidarity.

Deleuze and Guattari write about friendship in the introduction to *What is Philosophy?*[11] What is friendship? It is the ability to create a common world, a world of ironic enunciations and ethical expectations. Friendship is the possibility of creating a common path in the course of time.

'Caminante, no hay camino, se hace camino al andar.'

There is no path; the only path is our walking together.

There is no truth; there is no meaning; but we can create a bridge beyond the abyss of the non-existence of truth.

'The best lack all conviction' means: the best

have irony, the non-assertive language that aims to tune into many levels of meaning.

The ironic smile also implies empathy, ability to share life's precariousness without heaviness. When irony separates from empathy, when it loses the lightness and the pleasure of ambiguousness, then it turns into cynicism.

If irony is dissociated from empathy and solidarity, depression takes hold of the soul and irony turns into cynicism.

From a semiological point of view, we may see a similarity between cynicism and irony. In fact, cynicism and irony share the assumption that truth does not exist. But this is not enough. If we go beyond semiology, we understand that cynicism and irony differ at the ethical level. The ironic person is someone who does not believe in an absolute truth, but grounds her understanding on the empathic perception of the other, while the cynical person is someone who has lost contact with pleasure and bends to power because power is his only refuge. The cynical person bends to the power of reality, while the ironic person knows that reality is a projection of the mind, of many interweaving minds.

Different ethical stances emerge from the

philosophical understanding that God is dead and there is no metaphysical foundation of our interpretations and our discourses.

One stance is based on the violent enforcement of the *Wille zur Macht*. There is no truth in the world, but I'm stronger than you, my strength is the source of my power, and my power will enforce the truth.

Irony implies a different stance: we know that there is no ontological ground granting a common basis of truth, but friendship can build a bridge of meaning over the abysmal non-existence of meaning.

Gestalt, Tangle and Chaos

Our present impotence has been the perspective for my reflections in this book.

Our cognitive activity is encapsulated in the connective syntax, and the collaboration of millions of cognitive workers worldwide is entangled in the algorithmic form, of capitalism: knowledge and technology are directed and contained by the dominant paradigm, the gestalt.

The gestalt is not merely a form, it is a form that generates forms according to the gestalt itself. The gestalt gives us the possibility of seeing a certain shape in the surrounding flow of visual impulses, but by the same token the gestalt forbids us to see something else in the same flow of visual impulses.

The gestalt is a facilitator of vision, and simultaneously a disabler of vision (and generally of perception).

Our present political problem can be described in terms of the gestalt, of entanglement and disentanglement: how can the living intelligence disentangle itself from the algorithm and eventually reprogram the algorithm itself?

In the last chapter of their last book, *What is Philosophy?*, devoted to chaos and the brain, Deleuze and Guattari speak about ageing. Growing old essentially means being invaded by chaos: the ageing brain grows unable to elaborate the surrounding chaos. Better, the ageing brain grows unable to recognize order in the environment, and consequently perceives it as chaos.

Too fast, too fast: the infosphere around my brain is going too fast for emotional and critical elaboration.

As people live longer, with the remarkable exception of Islamic countries and Africa, in a large part of the world senescence is spreading, and senility is the psycho-cultural background of our society.

In the white Western part of the world, reproduction is slowing and slowing, and the demographical decline of the white race partially explains the mounting wave of reactive supremacism.

In order to heal the impending trauma, in order to overcome the post-traumatic effects of the impending apocalypse, we must shift the focus of our theoretical attention from the sphere of politics to the sphere of neuroplasticity.

Political action has to be replaced by a neurological reshuffling of the general intellect, with the activation of a technical platform for self-organization of cognitarians, and the reorientation of semio-production according to social needs.

I name this perspective 'the second coming of Communism'.

Capitalism is not a natural given; it is made insurmountable by our inability to imagine. We can't imagine Communism, only because our imagination is trapped by cynicism.

You can't imagine how beautiful life can be.

Believe me, I know by experience how beautiful life can be.

Greed, conformism, cynicism and ignorance are thwarting and dwarfing our ability to imagine and to live the imagination.

This is why I suggest you predispose your mind to the second coming.

Notes

How To

1 Gilles Deleuze and Félix Guattari, *What is Philosophy?*, trans. Hugh Tomlinson and Graham Burchell III (New York: Columbia University Press, 1992), p. 203.
2 Karl Marx, *Theses on Feuerbach* (1845), trans. Cyril Smith, https://www.marxists.org/archive/marx/works/1845/theses/index.htm, 2002.
3 Karl Marx, 'The Fragment on Machines', from *The Grundrisse*, pp. 690–712, http://thenewobjectivity.com/pdf/marx.pdf, n.d.
4 Crispin Sartwell, 'History, Totally Destroyed', *New York Times*, 11 November 2017.
5 Niccolò Machiavelli, *The Prince*, trans. N. H. Thomson (New York: Dover, 1992).

Chapter 1   In Retrospect

1 Max Roser and Esteban Ortiz-Ospina, 'Literacy', *Our World in Data*, https://ourworldindata.org/literacy, 2018.
2 Max Roser and Mohamed Nagdy, 'Projections of Future Education', *Our World in Data*, https://ourworldindata.org/projections-of-future-education.
3 Michel Foucault: *La naissance de la biopolitique: Cours au Collège de France, 1978–1979* (Paris: Seuil, 2004).
4 Melissa McEwen, 'I Just Don't Want To Be a Software Developer Anymore', *Medium*, https://medium.com/@melissamcewen/i-just-dont-want-to-be-a-software-developer-anymore-a371422069a1, 2017.
5 Reuters, 'Rodrigo Duterte Jokes to Soldiers that They Can Rape Women with Impunity', *Guardian*, 27 May 2017, https://www.theguardian.com/world/2017/may/27/rodrigo-duterte-jokes-to-soldiers-that-they-can-women-with-impunity.
6 Zbigniew Brzezinski, 'Toward a Global Realignment', *American Interest*, June 2016.
7 Michel Foucault, *Histoire de la folie à l'âge classique* (Paris: Gallimard, 1972).
8 Zafer Aracagök, 'Nonconceptual Negativity: Adorno+Life+Deleuze', *Non-copyriot.com*, 20 July 2017.
9 Karl Jaspers, *Die Schuldfrage* (1946; Munich: Piper, 1999).
10 Günther Anders, 'We, Sons of Eichmann: An Open Letter to Klaus Eichmann', trans. Jordan Levinson, *Anticoncept*, http://anticoncept.phpnet.us/eichmann.htm?i=1, 1964.

11 Konrad Paul Liessmann, 'Thought after Auschwitz and Hiroshima: Günther Anders and Hannah Arendt', *Enrahonar*, 46 (2011), 123–35, p. 127.
12 Günther Anders, *Die Antiquiertheit des Menschen, I: Über die Seele im Zeitalter der zweiten industriellen Revolution* (Munich: C. H. Beck, 2002), p. 291; quoted in Liessmann, 'Thought after Auschwitz and Hiroshima', p. 127.
13 Bernd Mayerhofer, 'Günther Anders: Existential "Occasional Philosophy" with a Critical Approach', trans. Jonathan Uhlaner, Goethe Institut, https://www.goethe.de/en/kul/wis/20365610.html, n.d.
14 Alfred de Gobineau, *Essai sur l'inégalité des races humaines* (Paris: Firmin-Didot Frères, 1853).

Chapter 2 Apocalypse

1 Niccolò Machiavelli, *The Prince*, trans. N. H. Thomson (New York: Dover, 1992).
2 Michael Hardt and Toni Negri, *Empire* (Cambridge, MA: Harvard University Press, 2000).
3 Hardt and Negri, *Empire*, p. 167.
4 Hardt and Negri, *Empire*, p. 41.
5 Hardt and Negri, *Empire*, pp. 182, 180.
6 Alain Joxe, *L'empire du chaos: Les Républiques face à la domination américaine dans l'après-guerre froide* (Paris: La Découverte, 2002).
7 Simon Nora and Alain Minc, *L'informatisation de la société* (Paris: Seuil, 1978).
8 Philip Howard, *Pax Technica: How the Internet of*

NOTES TO PP. 72–88

Things May Set Us Free or Lock Us Up (New Haven: Yale University Press, 2015), p. xiv.
9 Keller Easterling, *Extrastatecraft: The Power of Infrastructure Space* (London: Verso, 2014).
10 Easterling, *Extrastatecraft*, p. 15.
11 Easterling, *Extrastatecraft*, p. 11.
12 Easterling, *Extrastatecraft*, p. 13.
13 Easterling, *Extrastatecraft*, p. 14.
14 Easterling, *Extrastatecraft*, p. 92.
15 Easterling, *Extrastatecraft*, p. 137.
16 John Branch, Serge F. Kovaleski and Sabrina Tavernise, 'Stephen Paddock Chased Gambling's Payouts and Perks', *New York Times*, 4 October 2017, https://www.nytimes.com/2017/10/04/us/stephen-paddock-gambling.html.
17 Sheela Kolkhatkar, 'The Cost of the Opioid Crisis', *New Yorker*, 18 September 2017.
18 Theodor W. Adorno and Max Horkheimer, *Dialectic of Enlightenment: Philosophical Fragments*, ed. Gunzelin Schmid Noerr, trans. Edmund Jephcott (Stanford: Stanford University Press, 2007).
19 Herbert Marcuse, 'Repressive Tolerance', in Robert Paul Wolff, Barrington Moore, Jr, and Herbert Marcuse, *A Critique of Pure Tolerance* (Boston: Beacon Press, 1969), pp. 81–123.
20 Caitlin Dewey, 'Facebook Fake-News Writer: "I Think Donald Trump is in the White House Because of Me"', *Washington Post*, 17 November 2016.
21 Zeynep Tufekci, 'Mark Zuckerberg is in Denial', *New York Times*, 15 November 2016.
22 Kenan Malik, 'Gatekeepers and the Rise of

Fake News', *New York Times*, 5 December 2016.
23 Byung-Chul Han, *In the Swarm: Digital Prospects*, trans. Erik Butler (Cambridge, MA: MIT Press, 2017), p. 3.
24 Han, *In the Swarm*, p. 10.
25 Han, *In the Swarm*, pp. 5–6.
26 Dewey, 'Facebook Fake-News Writer'.
27 Jonathan Franzen, *Purity* (New York: Farrar, Straus and Giroux, 2015).

Chapter 3   Is There Life after the Apocalypse?

1 Nick Land, 'The Dark Enlightenment', http://www.thedarkenlightenment.com/the-dark-enlightenment-by-nick-land, n.d., p. 1.
2 Land, 'Dark Enlightenment'.
3 Jack Goody, *The Domestication of the Savage Mind* (Cambridge: Cambridge University Press, 1977).
4 Michel Foucault, *Histoire de la folie à l'âge classique* (Paris: Gallimard, 1972).
5 'Here there is no why': a Nazi concentration camp guard's reply to Levi's question 'Why?' Primo Levi, *Se questo è un uomo*, translated as *If This Is a Man* (London: Abacus, 2004), p. 35.
6 In 'Goodbye to the Mezzogiorno': 'though one cannot always / Remember exactly why one has been happy, / There is no forgetting that one was.'
7 Geert Lovink and Marc Tuters, 'They Say We Can't Meme: Politics of Idea Compression', *Net Critique*, http://networkcultures.org/geert/2018/02/11/

they-say-we-cant-meme-politics-of-idea-compression-geert-lovink-marc-tuters, 2018.
8 Marshall McLuhan, *Understanding Media* (Abingdon: Routledge, 2001).
9 Kevin Roose, 'Facebook Is Complicated. That Shouldn't Stop Lawmakers', *New York Times*, 11 April 2018.
10 Roose, 'Facebook Is Complicated'.
11 Gilles Deleuze and Félix Guattari, *What is Philosophy?*, trans. Hugh Tomlinson and Graham Burchell III (New York: Columbia University Press, 1992).